SHAPING
FORMLESS
FIRE
DISTILLING THE QUINTESSENCE OF MAGICK

Some Other Titles From New Falcon Publications

Aha! The Sevenfold Mystery of the Ineffable Love
–Aleister Crowley
Bio-Etheric Healing **–Trudy Lanitis**
Undoing Yourself With Energized Meditation and Other Devices
Secrets of Western Tantra: The Sexuality of the Middle Path
Dogma Daze
–Christopher S. Hyatt, Ph.D.
Rebels & Devils; The Psychology of Liberation
–Edited by Christopher S. Hyatt, Ph.D.
Aleister Crowley's Illustrated Goetia
Taboo: Sex, Religion & Magick
Sex Magic, Tantra & Tarot: The Way of the Secret Lover
–Christopher S. Hyatt, Ph.D., and Lon Milo DuQuette
Pacts With The Devil
Urban Voodoo: A Beginner's Guide to Afro-Caribbean Magic
–Jason Black and Christopher S. Hyatt, Ph.D.
The Psychopath's Bible
–Christopher S. Hyatt, Ph.D., and Jack Willis
Ask Baba Lon **–Lon Milo DuQuette**
Aleister Crowley and the Treasure House of Images
–J.F.C. Fuller, Aleister Crowley,
Lon Milo DuQuette and Nancy Wasserman
Enochian World of Aleister Crowley
–Lon Milo DuQuette and Aleister Crowley
Info-Psychology
Neuropolitique
The Game of Life
What Does WoMan Want? **–Timothy Leary, Ph.D.**
Rebellion, Revolution and Religiousness **–Osho**
Reichian Therapy: A PracticalGuide for Home Use
–Dr. Jack Willis
Woman's Orgasm: A Guide to Sexual Satisfaction
–Benjamin Graber, M.D., and Georgia Kline-Graber, R.N.
Shaping Formless Fire
Seizing Power
Taking Power **–Stephen Mace**
The Illuminati Conspiracy: The Sapiens System
–Donald Holmes, M.D.
The Secret Inner Order Rituals of the Golden Dawn
–Pat Zalewski
Sufism, Islam and Jungian Psychology
–J. Marvin Spiegelman, Ph.D.
Nonlocal Nature: The Eight Circuits of Consciousness
–James A. Heffernan
on What is **–Ja Wallin**

Other Titles by Dr. Israel Regardie

A Practical Guide to Geomantic Divination - A Small Gem
Attract and Use Healing Energy - A Small Gem
Be Yourself - A Guide to Relaxation and Health
Dr. Israel Regardie's Definitive Work on Aleister Crowley,
The Eye In The Triangle
Healing Energy, Prayer and Relaxation
How To Make and Use Talismans - A Small Gem
My Rosicrucian Adventure
Teachers of Fulfillment
The Art and Meaning of Magic - A Small Gem
The Body-Mind Connection, A Path to Well-Being - A Small Gem
The Complete Golden Dawn System of Magic
The Eye in the Triangle: An Interpretation of Aleister Crowley
The Garden of Pomegranates
The Golden Dawn Audio CDs
The Legend of Aleister Crowley
The Middle Pillar
The Portable Complete Golden Dawn System of Magic
The Tree of Life
The Wisdom of Israel Regardie - Vol. I
Selected Introductions, Prefaces and Forewords
The Wisdom of Israel Regardie - Vol. II
Selected Essays and Commentaries
What You Should Know About the Golden Dawn
Roll Away The Stone/The Herb Dangerous
(Dr. Israel Regardie and Aleister Crowley)

International Standard Book Number: 1-56184-238-9
Library of Congress Catalog Card Number: 2005929464

New Falcon Publications First Edition 2005
Second Edition 2010
Third Edition 2019

To contact the Author write to:
Stephen Mace, P.O. Box 256, Milford, Connecticut 06460-0256 U.S.A.

Those expecting a reply should enclose a stamped, self-addressed envelope.
Foreign correspondents should enclose international reply coupons.

The paper used in this publication meets the minimum requirements of the American National Standard for Permanence of Paper for Printed Library Materials Z39.48-1984 Printed in USA

NEW FALCON PUBLICATIONS
2046 Hillhurst Ave., Room 23
Los Angeles, CA 90027
www.newfalcon.com
email: info@newfalcon.com

By Stephen Mace

NEW FALCON PUBLICATIONS
Los Angeles, California

Table of Contents

Table of Contents
Continued

For
Barbara

Introduction to the First Edition

Magick depends upon no abstract philosophies, and doing it requires neither devotion to any god or demon nor knowledge of the True Keys of the Mysteries. Instead it is a technique for recognizing and manipulating psychic energy, both within the psyche and outside it, and for acquiring the mental skills we need to do this effectively. If the details of this technique can seem involved, well, the psyche is a complicated instrument, and psychic energy is slippery stuff to deal with. We must learn to manage it within our psyches and also to split it off so it can act independently to produce the "meaningful coincidences" we require. Also, it is what animates mind, so if it is given a focus for identity–even an artificial one–it can take on a mind of its own, and keeping that tendency in check adds to the complexity. And we need to consider the power in the world around us, and the ways we may take it in for our own use. So even if magick doesn't need to be so very complicated in the details, there's still a lot of ground to cover, and the subject can seem a bit daunting.

One difficulty in learning about it has been a dearth of concise introductions explaining just what magick *as such* is precisely about. There are plenty of advanced texts, of course, and many surveys full of generalities, but little that reduces it to the fundamental dynamics out of which the actual techniques are derived. Any text that attempts this should make the behavior of psychic energy clear and offer a few basic ways to exploit it safely, and this without requiring the reader to master any elaborate symbolic architectures or esoteric philosophies.

This book is built upon a series of ten essays that appeared in 2002-2003 in the German Wave-Gothic music magazine ***Zillo***[1]. Given the opportunity to write a page each issue for ten issues, I was obliged to break magick down into ten separate aspects–beginning with an explanation of what psychic energy does and moving on to what we can do with it, how we can keep it under control, the ways we can manipulate it, and finally a perspective on why we must. When it came time to bring these out in book form, it was clear there was room to go more deeply

[1] In this edition these are chapters I through IX, and XVII.

into the details without risk of clutter, and so I add six more chapters ranging in subject from curses and magickal morality to using sex in ritual–I hope in a style as spare as the original ten.

The reader reaction to the ***Zillo*** series was muted, which is just as well, the decision to take up magick being a personal one, and best not shared. Even so, in the issue of October 2002 there was a letter of objection from someone who apparently had a Christian orientation. The editors offered me the chance to reply in the next issue, and I took the opportunity to make the following argument for the necessity of magick:

A Reply to Hodavja

I assume from the content and the citations in Hodavja's letter that he or she is a Christian. I would surely not disparage the power of Jesus of Nazareth, a revolutionary magician who allied himself with John the Baptist against the spiritual monopoly held by the Jewish Temple Establishment of the early Roman Empire. Jesus failed in his efforts against these opponents and was killed by their Roman masters, but still left us with the wisdom that we are all children of God, and that the Kingdom of God is within us all.

But I and most other magicians would add that this realm is ours only if we have the courage to claim it, and there are techniques for doing this safely. Thus I offer an introduction to practical magick, a technology for manipulating psyche to manufacture the circumstances we require.

Psychic energy is ubiquitous, and we do better to learn to manage it than to flutter like a leaf in its wind, blown about by every passion or fad that we might encounter. Of course in some situations there is a lot more psychic energy present than in others, and a Wave-Gothic concert can be intense to an extreme. The whole glamour of the scene emphasizes the occult, especially vampirism, and the rhythms that drive the music are derived from Nigerian rhythms specifically developed to induce possession by the Yoruba gods. Also, I might add that the ongoing interpersonal interactions have much in common with a seething cauldron of hormones. Thus my emphasis on the disciplines offered in Parts 5 and 6, which allow us to keep all psyche under the control of our wills, wherever these might lead us.

Of course from this some cowards may conclude that we should shun Wave-Gothic concerts, lest our poor souls be put in peril. A pox upon them! Consider such concerts to be mere trials by fire, worthwhile tests preparing us for the far greater peril that is to be ours in the coming century. The Old Order–with all its politics and religion, science and commerce–is dying. It cannot repair or improve itself because all its energy and technics are devoted to staying alive. If humanity is to avoid slipping back into the preindustrial ooze, it is up to us to spawn something new to replace it. This is no task for those who would put their faith in any Great Holy Other, instead of in their own psychic competence. I offer a technique for developing such competence that is not that different from any number of others. Choose one and do it! There is time, but not that much.

I might add that in the two years since I wrote this reply, nothing whatever has occurred to make me question this grim prognosis; I think you will understand if I say that the events of 2003-2004 have simply confirmed it. The senescence of the empire is palpable even as it assimilates the entire planet, leaving no place anyplace as refuge from its inevitable collapse. The only escape will be through dimensions Pax Americana is unable to encompass, realms lying *behind* the expanse of its military and commercial space.

Magick offers access to these unclaimed territories. Only if we dare to step into them can we leave the decay behind us, and make a new world.

2005

CHAPTER I

THE FORCE THAT **DOES MAGICK**

Magick is as old as man, but in the past century it has undergone a radical change in attitude and practice. Sorcery, conjuring, the solicitation and interpretation of omens—all these were once hidden within tribal mysteries and secret societies. Now they are available to anyone who wants them badly enough to do the work. Nor are the tasks especially hard to figure out. All you need to do is do them. Magick quits being complicated once you know that it is mostly about recognizing that there is an invisible *stuff* all around you, a power that animates the awareness of everything that is conscious–a stuff that I'll be calling "psychic energy." Being the energy that activates consciousness, it has an effect on all its aspects, and can even spawn physical events if it builds up a big enough charge. With practice we can perceive a psychic charge and produce one. We can read the currents of psychic energy that flow around us, and influence them to our benefit.

The stuff of magick is psychic energy. When it occupies an animal or plant or some other self-aware entity, it serves as the energy that animates that awareness. But psychic energy can be split off from consciousness, either accidentally or on purpose, and then it can produce events or insights that have been called "paranormal."

What actually happens in each case depends on the cause of the split. If it is because an unpleasant fact is being rejected or repressed, it may discharge as an omen. But when a sorcerer conjures 'energized enthusiasm' to intentionally focus psychic energy into a talisman, he splits the energy off into a magickally effective 'container' that can carry the power to a specific place or time. If all goes according to plan, it will then discharge as an event or inspiration that will help the sorcerer get what he wants.

Or if a child represses anger at his or her family, it can hatch out as a poltergeist–causing anything from falling glassware to moving furniture and spontaneous combustion.

But the results of psychic energy acting outside of consciousness don't have to be especially strange. As I said at the beginning, we live in a sea of psychic energy. If it isn't split off to discharge on its own, its actions won't seem all that out of the ordinary. Any rock & roll band will take in the energy its audience sends it in the form of the audience's *attention*, and the more enthusiastic this attention is, the better the band will play. Since it is the crowd's psychic energy the players are absorbing, it will naturally affect the ways they feel and think, inspiring a supreme self-confidence in their own ability to play–a feeling that they can do no wrong. And so will their music soar. But if there is some kind of disconnection–if the band is preoccupied with taping for a TV Special, or if the audience is bored, cold, wet or abused by dirty air and bad acoustics–then the players will be beset with hesitation and hindrance, and the music will suffer.

Another instance of giving psychic energy is healing. This could occur through the psychic manipulations of an energy healer like a Reike Master or as a result of the prayers of the patient's devout relatives, who may focus their attention through the lens provided by their favorite saints.

The most notorious exchange of psychic energy is vampirism. Whether his or her tools be sexual, emotional, religious or political, the vampire feeds directly from the victim's vital force, leaving the victim drained and exhausted.

None of these are seen to be especially magickal. Vampires, for instance, are as common as your husband's aunt Mary (who is never feeling "quite well") or the latest charismatic guru, rabbi, mullah or preacher of the Gospels.

On the other hand, magickal skills will help you do any of these more safely and effectively. There are ways to open energy centers within your body and use them to beam free energy to your favorite rock & roll star. There are magickal principles you may follow to better connect yourself to your patron saints or clean a patient's sickness off of you after you do a healing. Magick is thus a psychic technology. Magicians apply their art to the psychic power flows they encounter and do their best to enhance and focus these so they best promote their purposes.

Magick happens in many ways. In this issue I have mentioned omens, conjuring, poltergeists, and three types of energy transfer, including vampirism. In issues to come I will be dealing with each of these in detail, and also divination, power spots, astral projection and the political ramifications of the magickal art. And I'm sure we'll think of more topics as we go along. If you have any ideas, feel free to contact me here at ***Zillo***. I can't promise individual replies, but I'll try to answer any frequently asked questions in the columns that follow.

Thanks.

CHAPTER II
OMENS

Omens are events in the world around us that seem to comment on what we are either doing or thinking about doing. If we don't believe in omens, we'll dismiss these events as coincidences–that is, if we even notice them at all. But then we just miss out on their advice, which is invariably right to the point and precisely what we need to hear. If we didn't need to hear it so badly, there wouldn't be enough tension in the field of psychic energy to spawn the event. Thus when there is such a tension, and the omen occurs, it pays to listen.

The last omen I got made a mess all over the place, but it was easier to clean up than the mess I would have made if I'd ignored the message. I had received a letter from a Very Important Correspondent, who objected to something I had written in my last letter. Well, there were reasons why I had said it, and I felt I was justified. But while I was trying to think of a way to compose my rebuttal, I knocked over a vase of flowers and spilled rotten water all over myself–which was a perfect comment on what I would be doing if I kept pushing an unnecessary disagreement. Since I'm not usually that clumsy, while I was changing clothes I considered what I had been thinking about, thought of how my rebuttal could be misunderstood, and decided it wasn't worth the risk. Thus I accepted the omen and simply replied with an apology and the business at hand, keeping my justifications to myself.

It's easy to explain an omen like this. And the same dynamic applies to prophetic dreams, waking visions, and premonitions of all sorts. These are all things that even a mainstream psychologist can accept. The subject's conscious plans or expectations are inconsistent with what his or her unconscious knows is needed, and so the strain discharges as the psycho/physical event–a "Freudian slip." All he or she has to do is recognize the connection and the difficulty is made clear.

But it isn't always so easy to account for omens. In the case of the rotten water in my lap, my two minds and my clumsy hand were all part of myself, and so the necessary linkages are obvious. But sometimes the omen appears as a "random" event in the outside world. Such events should logically be beyond our personal feelings, and so the occasion takes on an occult flavor. This is especially the case with political omens, those which occur to mark the rise and fall of great empires. These do not occur very often, but when they do, they are usually given notice in the records of the day. Of course in our skeptical, "scientific" age, such omens are usually treated ironically when they occur, and so we can only acquire any sort of certitude after events prove them accurate. One such omen that has stood the test of time occurred just before the collapse of Soviet power in Europe, about six months before the fall of the Berlin Wall, when the Soviets decided to make their first unilateral withdrawal of armor from Eastern Europe. The NATO Powers were skeptical of the Soviets' sincerity, but Gorbachev went ahead anyway. Toward the end of April, 1989, the first thirty-one tanks were loaded onto railroad flatcars and shipped out of Hungary. In that this seemed to be an event of world-historical importance, one celebrity in particular did make an appearance–Ilona Staller, one-time porn star and, at the time, a member of the Italian Parliament. As *Time* Magazine (8 May 1989) described the occasion, the fully-clothed Staller posed for photographs with the Soviet officers, "and released a white dove of peace." However...

"Ominously, perhaps, the bird was crushed in the treads of a Soviet tank." (p. 42)

Here the omen was obvious even to the editors of *Time*, though what anyone could have done about it is anyone's guess. The problem at the time was to know where those tanks were going to crush peace. One could consider that they were going to do it in Hungary, or even to the West, but since the occasion for the crushed bird was their departure east, it seemed to me at the time that that was where the fighting would occur. And subsequent events have shown that that was in fact the correct interpretation. The Warsaw Pact broke up with hardly a shot being fired; the prospect for peace in Europe hasn't been so good since before the Franco-Prussian War. But who can doubt that those tanks saw action in Chechnya? And of course surplus Soviet tanks were the principle heavy weapon used during the war in Afghanistan.

But then what causal link could there be between the behavior of a bird in Hungary and the condition of Soviet political unity? It is here that our explanations become magickal. Even so, they are consistent with my explanation for the omen of the vase of flowers. Both with my rebuttal to my correspondent and with the idea of peace in our time, there was an inconsistency between an individual's intentions and the facts of the situation. What we have to do is expand our idea of Mind, liberating it from its confinement in nervous tissue so it can flow as psychic energy across the earth. It's here that magick breaks with straight science, but it's better for it.

According to the magickal view, Mind comes before the nerves and flesh that enable its manifestation in Matter. In fact, it is the organizer of life, rather than a side-effect of it (as many academic scientists would have us believe). Psychic energy is a product of our living metabolisms that animates Mind within Matter, raising consciousness from a stupor to heights of creative enthusiasm. It is most intense within animals, but still spreads out through plants and the rocks, air and waters. So this field of awareness is everywhere, but not just a uniform background. There are currents within it, concentrations of power–some connected to individual living beings, others coming from the collective consciousness of nations, ecosystems and so on. And if the flow between these is in anyway blocked, say by the collective delusion of a whole nation, events occur that relieve the strain, events that have meanings analogous to the source of the strain. These we see as omens.

Ms. Staller's dove of peace was inconsistent with those tanks' ultimate disposition. On a deep level of consciousness, everyone present knew this, and from this discrepancy came the tension that was the source of the omen. If it had been acknowledged that those tanks would probably be going back to fight, there would have been no dove, no discrepancy, and no omen.

Chapter III
CONJURING

In the last two issues I've written about psychic energy and omens. I explained omens by saying that when a charge of repressed psychic energy builds up, it will discharge as an event that appears to comment on whatever it is that people are so determined not to think about. Conjuring is what magicians use to exploit this same dynamic for their own benefit. The magician uses magickal techniques to *manufacture* a charge of psychic energy in the hope that it will discharge in a way that promotes his or her purpose. It's what we do when we intentionally inject tension into the ocean of psychic energy, tension that will release itself by causing "random" events in our lives–or random thoughts in our minds–that turn out to our advantage.

The way the magician manufactures the energy is through anything that excites his or her awareness—anything from a formal ceremony to sex or drugs or rock & roll. Acceleration (as with a roller coaster or Ferris wheel) works, and so does walking around an altar in a magick circle while vibrating the names of ancient daemons. One can even take the energy called up by feelings of anticipation or disappointment, anger or fear, use magickal techniques to purify it, and then direct it to increase the tension. So long as the magician can maintain the tension and give the energy the symbolic focus it needs to concentrate it onto the problem he or she wants solved, any method will do.

It's what magicians do with the energy once they've conjured it that turns it from mere excitement into a maker of magick. What a magician does is separate the power from his or her stream of consciousness, in one way or another making it into something alien and other. By doing so, the magician puts the energy in a place where it cannot easily dissipate, which it would do if it were available to energize his or her normal thought stream. The deeper down the magician puts it, the more apt it will be to discharge not as hope or fear, but as event–event from a source completely outside the magician's conscious control, but nonetheless helpful to his purpose. Ways to split off the energy include both treating it symbolically–which is usual in ceremonial magick–and repressing all thought of it, which is common in more freeform techniques. The essential thing is not to let it into consciousness, where it can dissipate in a few moments of over-excited fantasy.

This leaves us with the need to manufacture psychic energy specifically dedicated to our purposes. If we are doing a ceremonial working, we will explicitly declare this purpose in the form of an oath at the beginning of the ritual–for instance, "I will earn a living playing guitar." Then we will invoke a deity whose powers are appropriate to this goal–in this case Apollo, god of music, who is attributed to the Sun, which is attributed to the metal gold. By invoking this god we will for a short time become as if we were that being in our consciousness. In this heightened state we can focus its power into a talisman, a symbolically compatible object (for instance, it might be painted gold, and decorated with symbols of the sun) that will serve to carry the power to where it can do the most good. Thus we might want to wear it while we're recording a CD or playing at a significant venue, or perhaps we will decide to bury it in the lawn of our record company's corporate headquarters.

If a musical magician decides to do a working of this kind, he must first have all his tools in order. He needs a place to work where he will not be disturbed, and he must have his magickal weapons (wand, cup, dagger, pentacle), the finished talisman, and a black cloth to wrap it in once it has been charged. To begin he will perform a banishing ritual to cleanse his space of all distracting thought, and he will formulate his purpose by pronouncing the oath. And then he will invoke the sun and all the gods of the sun, especially Apollo, using dance and chant and poetry and song–whatever brings his mind to the most excited state that he is still able to control. At the climax of the ritual, when he is filled with solar power, he will focus all that enthusiasm into the golden talisman. He will do this both by visualizing the power filling it so it glows with a golden light, and also by using a physical gesture: the Sign of the Enterer, taking a step forward as he extends his arms so his hands meet in a point, the energy flowing out of his fingertips and solar plexus into the talisman. He will then pull himself back together with the Sign of Silence–standing erect with eyes closed, his right forefinger held to his lips–and wrap the talisman in a black cloth. This will insulate the charge during the final banishing and protect it from random attention and other psychic currents until he can put it to the most effective use.

As I said, this could be anything from wearing it at a significant gig to burying it in the record company's lawn. Of course if he did bury it, the thrill he would get from the risk of getting caught would add to the energy of the whole operation, so long as he didn't let it discharge by dwelling on the thought of it. Nor should he allow himself to indulge in self-congratulatory fantasies once he gets it planted. He should simply leave the scene as quickly as possible (leaving no traces), find an open diner, buy a newspaper, and read it while he eats something greasy. By the time he's finished, the magick will be a distant memory, buried deep where its energy will ripen until it spawns the events he may grab for his own to pull himself up to that Olympus where guitar heroes never die.

CHAPTER IV
DIVINATION

We could sum up divination by saying that it's what we do when we conjure for an omen. For this we take up our bags of runes, Tarot decks or I Ching coins and use them to produce symbols that we may interpret in the light of our situations and the questions we're asking about them. And so we come up with an answer, generated by a method that is apparently random, but one that often enough produces strikingly relevant information.

Whenever we need to know how the psychic waves are moving, divination is the way to find out. Should we get married? Should we study medicine? Can we make Billy love us? What does out supervisor actually *want*? The answers to all these are better given in terms of awareness than of stuff, and so it would seem reasonable to search out an omen to show us the power flows active at the moment. But omens only come when they want to, especially since they need a certain amount of energy to cause the natural world to spawn an articulate event. After all, some fairly significant force has to cause the white dove of peace to fly down into the treads of the tank instead of up into the trees where it belongs. So instead of waiting for and hoping to get enough energy to move the natural world to action, we provide an artificial world that is far more sensitive to the weaker tensions we have available to move it, and this artificial world is the medium of divination.

The prime characteristic of any medium of divination is that it is a random symbol generator. Tossed coins or shuffled cards produce a selection of symbols from the all-inclusive system that is the oracle itself. What these systems will always attempt to do is to include, more or less precisely, all the more conspicuous dualities we meet within our lives–yes/no, love/hate, wealth/poverty, birth/death–and on to ever finer levels of exactness, depending on the number of symbols the medium of divination has available to explain its meaning. Thus when we flip a coin we have yes or no, but there are 78 Tarot cards and 4096 possible I Ching hexagrams, and both Tarot and I Ching are capable of generating an oracle after a few manipulations. We assume that the psychic stress carried by our question is sufficient to sway the feather of chance in such a way that the cards or coins produce a meaningful answer. Once this happens a few times, we may begin to take it seriously, and so do we acquire divination as our faithful tool.

The two things you must learn in order to divine correctly are 1.) the symbols that make up your chosen oracle's vocabulary, and 2.) an attitude. Learn the symbols by memorizing them from the book you buy with the oracle. The attitude to take goes something like this:

Treat the oracle as a wise advisor, an independent intelligence who inhabits the cards or coins and speaks in terms of the symbolic universe that the oracle represents. You must always treat it with respect, yet also with caution, never leaving any ambiguity in your questions, since from indefinite questions come unreliable answers. Of course part of treating an oracle with respect consists of not allowing it to be assaulted with unwarranted skepticism. If acquaintances seek to test it with any instrument sharper than an open mind, politely discourage their interest. If they expect it to give identical answers to repeated questions, then they have no idea how oracles work. The very act of asking the first time discharges the energy that gives the question its tension, and so removes the force that can move the oracle in a meaningful way. Hence obsessive questioning over the same subject only brings hotchpot and confusion, since the only force remaining to move the oracle is the anxious concern of the person doing the divining.

This leaves us with the question of what we can reasonably expect the oracle to actually do. In my experience what oracles do is show us the nature of the subtle currents that are active *right now*. They have no ability to precisely predict the future, because the future is a work in progress, subject to change without notice. Instead oracles indicate the nature of the power flows that are contributing to this process at the specific time that we ask the question. These power flows can change because other circumstances intervene, or we can change them ourselves by changing our attitudes or our actions in response to the oracle's reply. And this is the whole point of asking to begin with. After all, if the future were set in stone, no matter how accurate the oracle it would not matter, because we couldn't do anything about it anyway.

Thus it is always better to repeat our divinations from time to time as the moment for action approaches, and also before we conjure. In this way we make sure we don't put power into a situation that can't handle it, and so disturb a process that might work out perfectly well without our intervention. Conversely, once we do conjure, it is unwise to divine to ask how it went. The energy that the oracle uses to produce the answer is the very same energy that would go to produce our result, if we weren't so foolish that we wasted it through indulgence in reassurance. The best thing to do after you conjure is to forget that you conjured at all.

Chapter V
KEEPING CLEAN

So with omens, divination and conjuring we deal with psychic energy, either to discover its currents or manipulate them, and in this way we gain the knowledge, joy and power to lighten our ways through the world. But the first thing to learn about dealing with psychic energy is how to clean it off of you. Otherwise you will have it stuck on you from the first time you use it, and in time you won't know your own mind from the mind all around you, so mired in it all you will be.

Psychic energy sticks to us all the time. Whether we call it up with our own emotional responses to memories or events, or it attaches itself to us from the outside by means of fads, fashions or the enthusiasms of a crowd, psychic energy constantly animates our thoughts and feelings in ways that have nothing to do with what we want in the world. Since so much of magick involves focused thought, we need to get rid of these intrusions before we do any magickal work. Whether it involves divination, conjuring, astral projection, or contacting elementals in the landscape, our attentions are what both supply the energy for the operation and also direct it, so they had better be free of extraneous crap. And after the working is over, it's essential to have a tool to sweep away whatever is left of what we have called up.

What magicians use for both these tasks are what we call banishing rituals.

Banishing rituals are designed to send a stream of psychic energy out through the magician's consciousness and into the space around him, a stream that burns away any residue of thought that has stuck to him, no matter what its origin. The function of a banishing ritual is to clean out **everything** of a mental nature, leaving the magician with an awareness empty of all thought, with only his will remaining to guide him in his purpose. Thus the diviner's mind is cleared of everything but his or her question so that the oracle is not confused by any extraneous considerations. Thus the conjurer's mind becomes an empty vessel into which he or she may call up whatever pure power he or she needs to invoke for the purposes of the conjuration. And when the conjurer is finished and the power has been focused into the purpose of the working, the final banishing serves both to remove any residue, which could possibly blossom into an obsession, and also to put the fact of the operation out of the conjurer's mind, this allowing the energy to fester in darkness where it can grow into something inevitable.

But banishing rituals also have another, more long-term function. Through their habitual repetition (three or four times a day for the rest of your life), they build up your aura so it becomes impervious to external psychic currents unless you deliberately choose to let them influence you. Then whether you banish on any particular occasion or not, you will find yourself less susceptible to fads, authority, the enthusiasms of crowds, and the beliefs imposed by politicians, advertisers, and consensus reality in general. Such a diamond-hard aura will allow nothing but your own will to influence you as you create the reality you need to carry you through life.

Banishing rituals range from the simple to the symbolically elaborate. The one I give here is one of the simplest, but if you can concentrate on visualizing the lines, it can be as effective as the most complicated. Also it is easy to memorize and can be performed in your imagination in a few seconds, so it isn't very hard to make it a habit.

To begin, concentrate your thought in the point of view between your ears and behind your eyes.

Imagine a vertical line of light passing through it from beneath your feet to about ten centimeters above the top of your head.

Imagine a spot of light about thirty centimeters in front of your point of view. Use this spot to trace a circle of light around your head.

Then use it to trace an ellipse from in front of your face, over the top of your head, down your back, under your feet, and up the front of your body to the top of your head.

Finally, use it to trace a third ellipse down the right side of your body, under your feet, and up the left side to the top of your head. You should now be in the center of a cage of light that looks something like this:

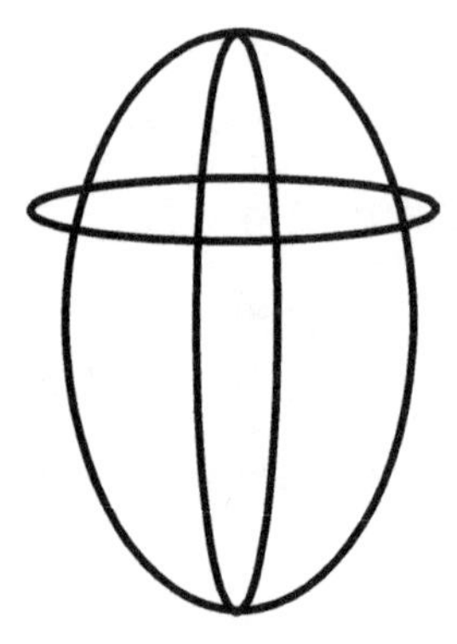

With your defenses in place, all you need to do is burn out your aura. To do this, transform the vertical line you first visualized into a pillar of fire. Let it expand out through the three rings, burning up any and all thoughts and images until there is nothing left but the three rings glowing blue-white.

This basic ritual may be made more elaborate as you gain competence as a magician. First of all, the ritual will acquire more punch if you use a consecrated dagger to trace out the rings, instead of merely visualizing them. And as you gain experience, you will invent words of power to enhance the cleaning and will also discover circulations of energy–especially those involving the Kundalini serpent–whose activation can empower the centering and cauterizing effects. But this advanced work will be possible only if you make the basic form of banishing a habit. By doing so, you prepare the way to transform your person into a fit tool for dealing with psychic energy. Without such a tool you can hope for neither safety nor advancement in the sorcerous path.

Chapter VI
YOGA AND SUCH

Psychic energy is what makes magick work, and to work magick we have to be able to manipulate it. We manipulate psychic energy with our minds, specifically the imagination and the subconscious. We deal with our imaginations with directed imagery. We deal with the unconscious through astral projection and repression. These require more than just a mind banished of clutter, but one that can concentrate on a thought without slipping into daydream or panic, silliness or spite. It requires the strength to repress all thought of something that only a moment before had filled your mind with energy.

I will offer two approaches to preparing the mind for magick. The first is meditation or yoga, but I won't get into that too deeply because there are so many other ways to learn about it. The second is a nasty little treat that Aleister Crowley offered in an instruction he called "Liber III vel Jugorum." This one is a little harder to find, so I will give you all you need to do it. It isn't long and it's easy to understand how it works. It's the doing of it that takes the fortitude.

The best yoga to train you for magick is called raja yoga. Aleister Crowley discusses it in detail in Part I of his *Book IV*, and I explain it in full in my *Stealing the Fire from Heaven*, published by Dagon Productions. Unlike yogas that concentrate on postures and movements, raja yoga only deals with training the mind. Thus its exercises are not as obvious as the more physical yogas, but that doesn't make them any easier. Not that the magician's training is very difficult when compared to the yogi's. Yogis usually try to use the exercises to attain Samahdi–conscious union with God. The magician doesn't have anything against Samahdi, but if he wants it, he's more likely to use magick to get it. That way he doesn't have to sit motionless for six hours each day for the rest of his life. Instead he'll have to sit still for about an hour and a half each day for about two years. Believe me, that is a big difference.

The major point of yoga for magick is to train your body, your breathing and your thoughts so they don't bother you while you're trying to do magick. This is especially important for astral projection, which is a sort of conscious journey into the unconscious, but it's also helpful for the various types of conjuring–just to train you to keep your mind on what you're doing. Here are some ways you can get started:

1.) **Posture.** You need to train your body so it doesn't bother your mind. To do this, simply sit in a chair with your back straight and your head erect. You can put a cushion on the seat, you can find the most comfortable place to put your hands, and so on. Then decide how long you're going to sit (fifteen minutes is good to start) and do so, without moving, until the time is up. Don't lift your hand to scratch your face. Don't shift your thighs to readjust your weight. Just sit until the time is up.

Of course you won't be perfect at the start. Your face will itch so much that you will scratch it. Your head will sag and you will straighten it again. This is understandable at the beginning, so it's nothing to worry about. The important thing is not to quit before the time is up. If you've decided on twenty minutes twice a day, sit for twenty minutes twice a day, and only sickness or the death of a near relation should be sufficient excuse to break your schedule.

The results here are remarkable. When you start the practice, it will seem easy. Then you will realize that it's only easy because you aren't doing it properly–which is to say, you'll be moving without realizing it. If you persist and correct yourself, you will succeed, but you will find that it hurts, and you will be so stiff when you finish that you'll have to take some minutes to stand up. But then if you still persist, you will reach a point where you can sit without moving and stand without pain. And so you will have succeeded, and the posture will be your tool for the rest of your life.

2.) **Breathing.** You can do this while you work on the posture. Simply breathe in to a count of four, hold to a count of four, breathe out to a count of four, and hold your lungs empty to a count of four. Don't breathe so deeply that you hyperventilate and fall over. Just make the pattern a habit so the need to breathe doesn't bother you anymore.

3.) **Concentration.** For this, simply visualize a simple object–say a red square. Do not let it change in shape or color. Do not let it sprout leaves or develop a background. Do not let it spawn thoughts of the Kremlin or Lenin's Tomb. At first you should be able to do this for about three-tenths of a second.

Keep at it, and at the end of the two years maybe you'll be up to five or ten seconds. But don't try too hard. It is possible to strain the mind.

Again, this is just a summary of a beginning. Go buy a book!

Crowley's "Liber III vel Jugorum" ("Book Three of the Yoke") is a bit different. It works to instill discipline in body, speech and thought through physical punishment. To do it, swear a formal oath not to perform a specific meaningless act for a specific period–say a week. Swear not to touch your face with your left hand. Swear not to say the word "for." Swear not to think about politics in the month before an election.

Of course you will break your oath, so a punishment must be specified. Since it must be convenient to repeat often (as often as three times in a minute if you've sworn not to say "and" or "I"), physical pain is about all that works. Crowley suggested cutting your arm with a straight razor, but that's just sick. Try stabbing yourself with a pin concealed in your clothing, snapping a rubber band worn around your wrist, or just bite your thumb! You can consider that you have succeeded with action, speech or thought when you have decreased your faults to one or two a day, and then when you've switched to a new prohibition of the same type, you still only commit one or two a day. Start with action and when you have mastered it, move on to speech. When you have succeeded with speech, move on to thought. When you have succeeded with thought, you can quit. But you will be different then.

To close I should stress that you must only forbid yourself meaningless things. If you forbade yourself the thought of how your parents liked your sister more than you, that would be repression, which all psychiatrists agree is a sure route to physical and mental illness. Instead you should strengthen your will on meaningless prohibitions so it becomes strong enough to deal with your psychic sore spots magickally. Then you will be their master instead of a victim pushing them out of sight, where they can only fester and turn rotten.

Chapter VII
CONJURING WITHOUT SYMBOLISM

In Part III–"Conjuring"–I wrote of using ceremonial magick to charge a talisman to bring a guitar player commercial success. Through his ceremony he creates an overabundance of psychic energy, an excess that he represses by focusing it into a talisman and burying it in his record company's lawn. By preventing the energy from discharging naturally as fantasy or loose talk, our musical magician obliges it to discharge "unnaturally" as an event that works to promote his purpose.

You may recall that I had our guitar-playing magician invoking Apollo, who also plays a stringed instrument (the lyre) and who is attributed to the sun, which symbolizes energy, gold, and the aspirations of the self. But there are dozens of other symbols evocative of music, money, and the sun that could be brought into this ritual, and of course the powers symbolized by the sun aren't the only ones you can use to do magick. There are also love and hate, logic and creativity, order and chaos–each with its own costume of symbols to specify its nature and suggest it to the mind of the magician. If you want to do ceremonial magick, you must assimilate these symbols completely–memorize them–and dress all your powers in the imagery they supply. Since power is unlimited, and the system itself is quite restricted, that is a distortion right there. The system will surely still work–they all do–but it will confine your progress to the tracks it has set down and you may not leave them without putting your power at risk. Since symbolism is necessary to specify the power our ceremonies call up, if we are to liberate ourselves from it, we must put ceremonial aside and find some other way to do magick.

Fortunately there is another way to conjure, a method which was the invention of the English artist and sorcerer Austin Osman Spare.

Spare's magick is based on two straightforward facts about psychic energy: 1.) psychic energy is freely convertible from one form to another, and 2.) if psychic energy is repressed, it will split off from self to act independently according to its own nature.

From these facts it follows that we should be able to take psychic energy directly from our daily lives and use it for conjuring, and that directing it to work magick could be as simple as then forgetting that we have ever done so. And this is just what Spare suggests.

For energy to be suitable for working magick, it must be free of any characteristics that would put it at odds with the purpose of the working, and the most obvious feature of such free energy is that it is silent. Energy that speaks as a voice in your head has a specific agenda from which the energy must be liberated before you can use it for conjuring. But inarticulate energy, whatever its source, may be used immediately, and you can find it in music, acceleration, dance, and sexual intercourse as well as through methods more strictly magickal. Or you can use magickal techniques to strip a more articulate sort of energy of its specific characteristics. Spare called the technique he offered for this "the Neither-Neither principle," based on "the dual principle," upon which manifestation itself depends.

The dual principle holds that there is no truth anywhere that is not balanced by an equally true opposite, and that the more you enforce one half of such a duality, the more necessary you make the other. To say that "up" exists makes it necessary for there to be a "down." To say that "life" exists requires that "death" be there as well. If it were not, we would not even notice life as a distinct state that needed to be specified.

To apply the Neither-Neither to do magick, simply wait until you have a strong belief in the truth of some proposition. Then force yourself to consider the truth of its opposite. If you can do this honestly, you will find your awareness flooded with an undefined energy, what Spare called "free belief." If there is a residual thought remaining, find its opposite and repeat the process, and again until there is nothing left but free belief and the empty mind that holds it.

Once free belief has been obtained it should be immediately focused into some magickal purpose. What Spare suggested was using it to concentrate on an alphabetic sigil–a monogram of your desire. To design one, simply write out your desire in a concise sentence, remove the duplicate letters, and make a design out of the ones remaining. For instance, the sentence could read: *I will earn my living playing guitar.* So we have the letters

IWLEARNMYVGPUT.

Out of these (if we permit rotation) we can make this sigil:

When free belief or any other inarticulate energy[2] is present in your mind, use it to visualize your sigil. Make it glow bright in your mind's eye and keep it glowing until the energy is exhausted. When the sigil fades, put it out of your mind and do not allow yourself to think of it until you have more energy to put into it.

This brings us to the second fact of psychic behavior that Spare's method exploits: that if psychic energy is repressed, we split it off from us so it acts independently according to its nature. By using free belief to visualize the sigil, we give it the character the sigil defines. By repressing it we force it to act on its own. This repression has two aspects. On the one hand, you should simply not think too much about what you want. This is impossible to do perfectly,

[2] Orgasm, acceleration, release from danger, the admiration or applause of a crowd, catharsis from music or dramatic productions, catharsis from architecture or a landscape, etc.

since you must work for your goal on all planes. The magician who conjures to make a career in music must do music in all its aspects, and this will occupy his mind. But he should not fantasize about success while killing time in his mind-numbing day-job, or anticipate it while making small talk with his musical colleagues. Fantasy and small talk do nothing to push one's magickal purpose, and they waste power like a cheap drug.

The second aspect of the repression pertains to the magick, which must be completely stifled except when you are actually doing it. Never think of the sigil unless you have power ready to charge it. Never think about the magick unless you are actually planning to do it. And never think that you have done the magick until the result you require from it has occurred to your satisfaction.

Chapter VIII
ASTRAL PROJECTION

In Parts V and VI, I spoke of self-protection with banishing rituals, and self-control developed through the use of spiritual exercises. With these you gain the ability to clean out consciousness and manage its contents, at least for a little while. This was useful in Part VII, where we talked about conjuring by preventing our desires from entering our minds, and never thinking of our sigils except when we have energy to charge them. This control is also essential for the practice of astral projection.

Astral projection is the process of going onto the astral plane, where we may meet spirits both from within our own minds and also those that reside independently of them. Once they stand before us, we may discover their names and bind them to obedience, but when we do this we must be stronger than they are if we are to escape obsession by them.

The way we get onto the astral plane is through our own imaginations. Astral projection is a special type of meditation whose defining characteristic is a separation of bodies at the beginning of the projection, and their reunion at its conclusion. We use visualization to separate the astral body from the physical body and transfer our consciousness into the astral body. In this astral body we explore the astral plane, leaving the physical body essentially forgotten. When the projection is over, we must be careful to reunite our two bodies, superimposing the astral precisely over the physical, tightening all our muscles to seal the reunion, and then suddenly, as an act of will, *waking up*.

In sorcery the operating assumption is that any psychic characteristic–any talent, phobia, or habit of thought or behavior–may be characterized as a distinct spirit and manipulated as such through the techniques of sorcery. On the astral plane we meet these spirits face-to-face. Our astral bodies are sensitive to perceive them and to evoke them–either with traditional symbolism or with the method of alphabetic sigils that I offered in Part VII. The astral is the spirits' own territory, so they are more available to us there, but at the same time we make ourselves more vulnerable to them, so we need to have control right from the start. Traditionally you do this by forcing every spirit you deal with to acknowledge your authority. To accomplish this, recite a ritual charge to the spirit while it stands before you in your mind's eye. Such charges are written in formal language, long enough to make a demand on memory and concentration, but not so long that they are boring. The one I like is from Aleister Crowley's "Preliminary Invocation" from the *Goetia*, derived from a ritual originally written in the Egypt of the Roman Empire. The Charge to the Spirit goes like this:

> *Hear Me, and make all Spirits subject unto Me: so that every Spirit of the Firmament and of the Ether: upon the Earth and under the Earth: on dry Land and in the Water: of Whirling Air and of rushing Fire: and every Spell and Scourge of God may be obedient unto Me.*

On the astral we can meet any spirit that we can define as useful to us. Any power of mind or nature that we can recognize can be treated as a distinct spirit that we can name, bind, and conjure to help us do our wills. Powers of mind could include the ability to play the guitar or read other people's emotions, the power flows and power centers in our subtle bodies, demons like a tendency to indulge in conflict or self-pity, and even entities that we synthesize, for instance the spirit that transforms anger at the civil state into literary creativity. Powers in the outside world could include elementals like the spirit of a landscape or a building, or they could be independent intelligences like Aiwass, herald of the new aeon. (We'll be getting to him in Chapter XVII.) Astral projection is our tool to meet any of these and gain their allegiance. Once we have it we can call them up anytime we need them, whether we are on the astral or not.

Now with spiritual exercises like yoga and "Liber III" to build up our strength, it would seem that the domination of our spirits should be relatively easy. But strength cannot prevail against deception. Every spirit would love to make you believe that it has knowledge of and power over all things, instead of merely its own narrow area of specialization. Each would promise you all the power in the world if only you would allow it to take control over your will. But this is the way to madness and crime. To do this is to give a very small part of you control over the whole thing. It may indeed possess great power, but that doesn't mean it is competent to run your life.

It's for this reason that the testing of spirits is a crucial part of astral work. In traditional magick this is done by taking care that any spirit we meet wears the symbolic uniform of the power it claims to represent. With the freeform approach using alphabetic sigils, we must simply use the sigil to call the spirit up, and then see if it will tolerate the imposition of the sigil over its form in our minds' eyes.

Of course all this would be easier if you had an assistant on the planes to manage all the spirits you meet there. For this you have your Holy Guardian Angel, which might be seen as an astral foreman who has control over all the entities in your spiritual swarm. Traditionally the way to become acquainted with your Angel was through months of progressively greater austerities. An alternate method is to design an alphabetic sigil from the letters of a sentence requesting knowledge of it. Then after about six weeks of putting energy into it, you should be able to use it to meet your Angel on the astral. Your Angel will serve as an assistant who can call any spirit you require, give you its name, help you bind it, and back you up if it gives you any trouble.

To close I will simply observe the obvious–I have told you a great deal about astral projection, but I haven't given you the explicit instruction you need to do it. This is because its proper practice is just too complex to fit into the space I have here, this being a music magazine, after all, and not a journal on sorcery. But there are many books on the subject, including some of my own[3], and with this essay as background, you should be able to decide whether you wish to pursue it. But if you do, just remember these simple points:

Banish before and after every astral experiment.

Always close what you open, and put as much effort into binding yourself back together as you did splitting yourself apart.

The way back is the way you came.

[3] I give a complete treatment of the practice and theory of astral projection in the chapter "Astral Projection" in *Taking Power: Claiming Our Divinity Through Magick* (New Falcon Publications, 2005).

Chapter IX
ELEMENTALS AND POWER SPOTS

The basic assumption for the sorcerous approach to magick is that any aspect of your life or the world around you that you can define as distinct or separate will also have an ethereal aspect that you can define as a distinct or separate spirit. And once you define a spirit you can enter into a magickal relationship with it–conjuring it, naming it, and binding it so it obeys your will.

This applies to specific features of the external world as well as to aspects of our unconscious minds or independent spirits or demons on the astral plane. Each location, structure, or ecological or geological phenomenon will have a spirit of its own which the sorcerer may cause to assist him as its nature allows. Of course for the average spot on the surface of the earth, this will be in no special way at all. The location will be psychically dormant, with no knowledge and no power, one spot running into the next without any particular psychic distinction. On the other hand, there are significant locations scattered all around us that display their power to anyone who is looking for it. Rivers and ridgelines, hillocks and woodland glens, lakes and meadows and inland seas–all these can have a potential for providing knowledge and power that may be used to promote our purposes.

Of course recognizing a spot as worthwhile is one thing, meeting and naming and binding its elemental quite another. For a beginner to meet the spirit of a place requires that he or she undertake a full-scale astral projection, which is not all that difficult if the spot is somewhat isolated, especially at night. But with practice, and especially after you have become acquainted with your Holy Guardian Angel, an astral state of mind may be acquired through a simple meditation to enter into rapport with the location's mood. Once you enter this state of mind, ask your Angel the name of the spirit of the place and any details you need to evoke it, then use that name as a chant or mantra to call it to appearance in your imagination. When the spirit stands before you in your mind's eye, do all you can to perceive its essence, then gather it together to bind with a ritual charge. In Chapter VIII I described how we may use a ritual charge ("Hear me, and make all spirits subject unto me...") to control the spirits in our unconscious minds. Well, we must take the same precaution with elementals. The control you gain over the elemental will surely be more limited than what you could expect from a spirit residing in your own unconscious, but at least it will be sufficient to enable you to work with its power without risk of obsession.

Once the spirit of a place has been properly bound, you may rely on it for support within the realm of its competence. From an ocean you might obtain the power to attain your true level, which is to say, to accomplish your destiny. From a river you might take its implacable motion (especially if it's in flood), or the ability to perceive in at least a watery fashion over the extent of its watershed. An escarpment might provide you with the access it opens to the power at the center of the earth. An office tower might supply you with insight into the corporations that are its tenants, or assist you in getting a job or an account with one of them. Or you might use the spirit of a place to promote a mutually beneficial purpose. For instance, to cause your favorite musical group to play with greater skill and verve, you could call upon the elemental of the building they are playing in, and of the earth its foundations are sunk into (since discos are often in basements). This will give you an inspiring musical experience and also help the building pay its rent, thus keeping it from being razed to make room for an office tower.

Now any place potent enough to have a presence worth meeting may well include a power spot, a place no more than a few meters square where power can be absorbed directly from the spiritual fabric of the planet. Often these will be conspicuous from their incongruity, as with a spring out of a high rock or a rock formation in the middle of a marsh. Others will compel attention from their charisma, for instance a rocky seat set in the top of a cliff, or from their simple beauty. But even the subtle ones are easy enough to find if you ask the elemental of the overall locale. You can treat the energy emanating from a power spot as a spirit, asking your Angel to call it forth and tell you its name so you might bind it and use it as you can.

Spots vary in their dynamic characteristics as well. Depending on what sort it is, you might be able to pull energy out of it for later use, or perhaps it will serve as an entry way into the bowels of the earth into which you may place talismans so they will better accomplish your purposes. You may recall how, in Chapter III, I described how a person who wanted to make a living playing music could bury a talisman in his or her record company's lawn. Obviously the rationale here is that this is the way to get the power closest to those who can make the desired event happen. But I know of a cave in Connecticut where I can bury talismans and have them cause significant effects in Germany. Once you find a route to the center of the earth, the whole planet becomes available to you.

On the other hand, I should note that spots vary in their qualities from the entirely beneficial (whose power can be stored directly) to the pernicious (which should be avoided entirely). Even if the obvious differences in charisma don't give clear warning, your Angel will provide it, if only you think to ask.

Zillo being a European publication, I can't emphasize enough the importance of a knowledge of historical background when looking for significant locations. The seers of ancient Europe found many significant power spots a thousand years before Christianity outlawed all pagan practice, but the Christians couldn't stifle the spots themselves. So they built shrines to the Virgin or to whatever saint began to appear there after sensitive individuals learned how to interpret all power in terms of Christian symbolism. And from shrines came monasteries and cathedrals, and the towns that serviced them. So now you have some really significant sources of power decorated with some really nice architecture but also with some really inappropriate imagery (though with the Protestants one does occasionally encounter an Eye in the Triangle). It's best to just stand in awe of the architecture but let the saints and such fade into an incoherent blur of color as you go about your business of tapping the power there.

Consider it an exercise in concentration.

Chapter X

INITIATION AND MAGICKAL NAMES

Initiation means a beginning, and in the occult it is the occasion when one becomes aware that the world is more than just the material stuff within it. The stuff is merely the façade that lies over a churning sea of psychic energy, power whose currents and tides do more to determine how the material stuff will be arranged in the future than the stuff that is out there right now. Reality is the objective residue of a subjective process. The residue–the material world–has a certain inertia, to be sure; it won't just go away. But it does dissipate, decay, get eaten up and covered over, and it is only created anew when some mind of some sort–animal, vegetable or mineral–puts effort into that creation. And so does subjectivity make the world.

Magick is the art of managing that subjective process, of exploiting the flow of psychic energy to manufacture a reality that is consistent with our wills. A magician's first initiation occurs in the moment that he or she realizes that this manipulation of psychic energy *as a thing in itself* is possible.

Initiation of some sort is as old as mankind. The original initiations were puberty rites, wherein the youths in a tribe would be brought through painful ordeals and then taught the secrets of manhood, emerging into a new identity, often with a new, secret name. Such ordeals were more common for men than women, who must undergo the spontaneous ordeal of childbirth. But in both cases the initiate dies to the old life and is reborn in the new. Nor is the "death" entirely symbolic, since such ordeals as radical circumcision, hunting tests, ritual combat and, indeed, childbirth do carry a real risk of death. But they must be gone through if the death-in-life of the social outcast is to be avoided.

In tribal circumstances the initiation usually led to a glimpse of the spirit of the ecosystem from which the tribe won its sustenance. But once mankind had passed out of tribalism and into civilization, such glimpses became counterproductive. People no longer lived through their harmony with the earth, but instead with the sun. It was the solar year that one had to be in step with in order to properly exploit the ecosystem. So instead of the power behind all things, the secret to be realized was that of death and rebirth, a lesson that was given in the various Mystery Cults of dying and resurrecting gods: Orpheus, Isis and Osiris, Mithras, and even Christianity. All these had their rituals for initiation, wherein the new member was brought through a symbolic death and resurrection and then taught the hidden truths. Even Christian Baptism can be considered in such a light[4], though only in its adult usage. Infant baptism is the waste of a perfectly good ritual on those who would prefer to be sucking a soft, warm tit instead of getting their heads wet in a drafty old church.

In any event, the idea of occult initiation as it was used by the Mysteries underwent a rebirth during the Renaissance. It was incorporated into the Rosicrucian mythos and from there was established in the practice of Freemasonry. Here the theme was no longer life-death-resurrection in the literal sense, but a death to life in the mundane and a rebirth into the realm of Light and Truth. This is the form it took during the Rosicrucian Revival of the 19th and early 20th centuries. The candidate was bound, hooded, threatened with a sword, charged with Light by the

[4] See Romans 6:3-11.

membership and then released to receive the instruction appropriate to an initiate of the Order. And so it has continued to this day in formal occult usage.

But there is another sort of initiation we should mention, one where the initiate neither sets out to seek for knowledge nor is led into it by friends or lovers. Instead power sneaks up behind the initiate and pushes him or her into an awareness of it as if off a cliff into the sea. If the formal initiation is more measured, it also leaves one with the option of losing interest and sliding back into the mundane. The second leaves you with no options at all. You are hurled into an ordeal and either win through into an awareness of power, or else shrink back from it in the knowledge that your cowardice cost you a chance at a whole new world.

My own initiation followed this pattern. I was living in a university town, working at selling substances that the civil state, in its infinite ignorance, defines as contraband. One day an acquaintance told me of his interest in the magick of Aleister Crowley and, being somewhat skeptical, I asked for a demonstration. He suggested a Tarot reading and I accepted. The card for my immediate future was the Nine of Swords, which Crowley, in his *Book of Thoth*, entitles "Cruelty" and describes as representing the energy of the fanatic: "crude rage of hunger, operating without restraint. Though its form is intellectual, it is the temper of the inquisitor." Three days later the State Police broke down my door with a sledge hammer, pointed pistols in my face, tore my apartment to pieces, bound me with handcuffs, and locked me in jail for six weeks. The pistols provided a more credible threat than a ritual sword; the handcuffs were more painful than a velvet cord; and the jail was a worthy tomb/womb wherein I was put face-to-face with the worst of the demons in my psyche. When I got out it felt like a true rebirth. I returned to the gentleman who had given me the reading to ask him how he'd done it. Though he wasn't too clear on the specifics, he gave me the background I needed to pursue the quest on my own, and I've been at it ever since.

Whether a person's initiation be deliberate or spontaneous, it is customary upon its conclusion to take a magickal name. This name signifies the new initiate's entrance into magickal consciousness and is usually a motto epitomizing his or her view of his or her relationship with the universe thus revealed. The magician would use this name to refer to his or herself whenever he or she was acting in a magickal capacity. Magickal names were once far more important than they are now, when anonymity was necessary for survival, and they may still be convenient for that purpose. Ceremonial magicians may also use them to help keep magickal actions separate from their mundane lives, thereby effectively preventing their magickal energy from leaking into mundane consciousness. Thus the energy can better build up the potential necessary to cause the change the magician requires.

Generally magickal names are in a foreign language: often Latin, Greek, Hebrew, "Enochian" or a nonsense word somehow significant to the initiate. Aleister Crowley's name when he was initiated into the Golden Dawn was "Perdurabo," meaning "I shall endure unto the end." Austin Spare's motto was "Zos vel Thanatos," thereby mixing Latin, Greek, and his own magickal system. On the other hand, magickal names can be purposefully meaningless. Members of Thee Temple ov Psychic Youth, for instance, all call themselves either Kali (for women) or Coyote (for men), followed by a random number. The point here is to discourage all kinds of hierarchy and status seeking. The numbers are even recycled as membership changes. On the other hand, in hierarchal orders like Crowley's A.A., one would take a new motto as one rose into each new rank in the hierarchy. The idea here is that with each increase in rank one reaches a new level of magickal competence and insight, and thus would require a new motto to distinguish it. Thus Crowley could sign his writings "Aleister Crowley," "Frater Perdurabo," "OY MH" (Gk: "Neither-Not"), "V.V.V.V.V." ("Vi Veri Vniversum Vivus Vici," Latin: "By the force of Truth, I, while living, have conquered the Universe"), and "TO MEΓA ΘHPION" (Gk: "The Great Beast"), for the ranks of Man, Neophyte, Exempt Adept, Master of the Temple and Magus, respectively.

Crowley gives a thorough explanation of his hierarchy in "One Star in Sight," which is Appendix II of his *Magick in Theory and Practice*.

Chapter XI
WHITE MAGICK, BLACK MAGICK

We may dismiss "white magick" as that sort of occultism that is solely concerned with the goals of mysticism—meaning union with the Absolute, oneness with the Light, Nirvana, that sort of thing. This is indeed a possible course, but to my mind a rather premature enterprise. We all have now a body of flesh, and it seems most reasonable to use our magick to live more triumphantly through it. Union with the Absolute will come soon enough–they call it "death"–and then using magick in the material world will no longer be an option. But we might speculate that the skill we gain at manipulating power in this world may be to our advantage when we are faced with what comes in the next, when the self-control thus won could help us keep our coherence after our foundations in body have returned to the dust from whence they came.

The platitude of the "White Light" faction–condemning all magick done for practical purposes as "black magick" and stating that only "spiritual advancement" is a legitimate goal–is stupid. From a better job to an introduction to the love of your life, from courage in public speaking to the ability to do away with arrogance, any goal in magick that improves your circumstances without stealing from someone else's is legitimate. To say otherwise is simply spiritual snobbery, which is the most pernicious sort of arrogance of all.

Even so, when we do decide to apply magick to the outside world, the question of ethics does become unavoidable. Indeed, there are many people fascinated by the art who study it but dare not practice out of fear of descending into black magick, ultimately damning their souls to everlasting perdition, perpetual reincarnation as a lower life form, or whatever. This fear is not entirely unfounded, but is no more a risk in magick than in business, religion, politics, or interpersonal relationships. Magick is magick, just as money is money, civic authority is civic authority, and sex is sex. There is nothing wrong with any of them *as such*. The wrong comes from their improper application. The only thing that makes magick any different is that it is impossible for the police or the courts to punish the person who uses it for evil[5]. But this really matters very little, since retribution will come whether police and priests notice the evil or not. Retribution in magick has more to do with the laws of physics than those of God or government. And these laws may be summed up with one simple sentence:

You can't get something for nothing.

You can't get wealth without making it. You can't get devotion without giving it. You cannot curse without calling up a spiritual malignancy that in the end may cause you more grief than it does your opponent.

Take, for instance, the use of magick to get money. There are two ways to go about this. You can either conjure to create a life situation where you will earn it by doing things you enjoy, or you can just conjure for cash. If you choose the first alternative, you will be using magick in the most positive way possible, producing value for which grateful patrons will pay you money. If you choose the second, you will be squeezing a few extra drops of value out of the fabric of Fate

[6] In this chapter my references to "black magick" refer only to using standard methods of conjuring to promote twisted ends. When one uses perverse methods of conjuring (human sacrifice, child rape, etc.), this does not even deserve the title "black magick," for it is no magick at all. It is just crime.

without any notion of where it will actually be coming from. And Fate always squeezes back.

Now it is a truism on all levels of action that the thing that moves most easily always moves first, and this certainly applies to the person who conjures for wealth without specifying any method for its production. That is, the wealth will come from the most immediately available source. Considering that the magician who conjures in this way probably doesn't have much else going for him, this value will most readily be found in the vast insurance pool that underlies modern society. Even if he has invested in no policy himself, and has no beloved relatives who have named him as their beneficiary, there is always the chance for a crippling accident caused by the inattention of a well-insured motorist. Then our magician may never want for anything else ever again, except for a left leg.

The same considerations apply to operations for love, and those of magickal combat. Magick for sex is not so dangerous, but conjuring to cause specific people to consent to intimacy is full of risk. Conjuring for sex is just doing magick to bring together like-minded people, and to adjust the conjurer's sensibilities so he or she is not too picky when these people appear. But if you are attracted to someone specific, and yet you are not now intimate, then there must be some reason why. Maybe she dislikes your body type, or perhaps he wonders about your husband. Maybe it's because you don't own a BMW, or perhaps he just isn't interested in women. Or she may just want to finish her university work, and would have you if you would only have the patience to back off and wait. But if you conjure to force such a person into your bed, such inhibitions will not be banished or resolved, but only momentarily overwhelmed. And then they will rise up redoubled to infest the relationship, and through it your whole life.

The alternative, as with the money magick, is to use magick to build what you want from scratch. Use it to meet a compatible partner, to obtain the sensitivity to read his or her expectations and moods, and to recognize your own alienating behavior patterns and work to redirect the energies that animate them. A certain sensitivity of purpose–both other people's and your own–is required to do magick. If you don't have one already, use magickal techniques to develop one before you begin to use them to manipulate your external circumstances.

Sensitivity, adroitness and a good eye for consequences are even more important for our third subject here–curses and magickal combat–to which we will direct our attention in the next chapter.

Chapter XII
CURSES AND MAGICKAL COMBAT

The essence of a curse involves the evocation of a demon of heart-rotting nastiness and setting it upon one's opponent, but as I said in the last chapter, it may come back. A good illustration of this process is given in a curse developed by Tzimon Yliaster called "The Conjuration of the Qisdygym."[6] In this ritual the sorcerer evokes the qisdygym out of a wooden bowl filled with polluted water and a drop of his or her own blood. Once the demon has been sent, the sorcerer hides bowl and water away, and waits.

This is where it gets difficult. Yliastar cautions that one must refrain from giving the qisdygym a name, or even thinking about it once one has sent it on its mission, since this will surely call it back to the person who conjured it, causing that person to "become its host and suffer its affections." Also, the sorcerer must be careful to monitor his or her

[6] Published in Widdershins 6, Santa Cruz, 1997, pp. 40-41.

victim's status, because as soon as the qisdygym has finished with the victim, it will return to the sorcerer, who may be unaware of its return "until it is too late."

Once the demon has done its work, the sorcerer must immediately banish while burning the bowl, and then quench the fire with the blood and water, thus destroying the qisdygym before it can return. Incidentally, Yliaster describes the qisdygym's action by saying that "it will cause whomever it is attracted to to make 'fatal errors,'" these generally consisting of "physical clumsiness or inappropriate reaction."

The key phrase here is "whomever it is attracted to," for the demon of a curse will attack its victim more through the victim's susceptibility to its morbid energies than by hurting the victim with its impact. And here the justification for the attack assumes great significance. If the target is essentially innocent, he or she will not be susceptible. The demon will have no access to this person at all, even as the curser (in the case of the qisdygym) must remain alert to burn and banish the bowl, even as he struggles not to think of why he must do so. If this went on long enough it could cause even the best developed concentration to crumble in the end, with potentially fatal results.

Thus we have the formal curse, the entity manufactured in some sort of ceremony to carry out the sorcerer's mission of extermination. But less formal modes of psychic attack and defense are also pertinent. One particularly foolish way to launch an attack is to simply send a stream of hate and anger out against an opponent. This is a favorite method of bullies in commerce and government who possess some psychic talent but no training in magick. Unlike the demon sent with a curse, the energy here strikes with impact, and it can be felt as a pressure on the aura that threatens to escalate into difficulty breathing. If one then panics, a trip to the emergency room is a likely outcome, followed by psychiatry and anti-anxiety medication. This sort of attack can indeed be effective when directed against a member of the human herd, but any sorcerer with astral competence will find it easy to counter. You can do this by having previously personified your own most aggressive qualities as a spirit, then naming and binding it, and thus having it ready to *eat* any energy sent at you with malicious intent, converting the energy into neutral magickal power.

With the assistance of your Holy Guardian Angel, the creation of such a spirit should take no more than an hour's astral work. It should be called up the instant you perceive you are under attack and directed to consume the stream of malignancy that you visualize as impacting on your aura. The spirit should set to with gusto, for pure hate and aggression are its main meat. You should allow it to keep chewing until it comes to your attacker's point of identity, where it should bite the extension off and return to you, its master. Ideally this will leave your attacker exhausted, full of fear, and possessed of a newfound humility rooted in his or her awareness of the extent of his or her magickal ignorance.

Such a defensive spirit differs from a demon like the qisdygym in that it is a part of your personality under your control, not any sort of independent horror called up for an attack. Also, you do not use it to assault another person, but simply to catch and eat the energy the other person uses to assault you. Hence you need not make a link to the other person, and there is no need to be concerned over his or her vulnerability. The other person has already made the link to you, and by attacking he or she is already as vulnerable as it is possible to be, just as a boxer must momentarily become defenseless whenever he throws a punch.

Of course curses are a rarity, and even attackers of the second sort are few and far between. During my whole occult career, I can't say that I have ever received a formal curse, and I've had to counter at most three of the streams of hostility just mentioned. But this does not mean that there isn't plenty of negative energy bouncing around the environment. There is, but we can't really call it occult. That is, it isn't hidden, but instead is delivered with what often seems like ostentatious display. Whether a haughty sales clerk or an obnoxious customer, a reckless driver or a loudmouthed pedestrian, the energy they emit will be psychic even if it isn't magickal, and so our psychic technology should be able to deal with it. And so it can. On the most basic level, we can manipulate our auras to better deal with negative energies. Obnoxious people tend to let their auras flame out and push in the auras of their victims; a simple activation of Kundalini and circulation of the Light will help you reinflate yours, and remove the need for the reflex of resentment. Or one can simply have a word to split off the aggressive response that they conjure, so the energy leaves you and goes...where?

Probably back to the one who conjured it in you. The procedure works great with tailgaters.

So where does one get such a word? By going onto the astral and calling up the power of severance, then embodying it as an entity, a separate spirit you can name and bind. It's not so hard as it sounds once you get up there, since the astral quite readily responds to any form you impose upon it. But you'll find it a lot easier to work with after you've become acquainted with your Holy Guardian Angel. Make it a priority!

Chapter XIII
THE SUBTLE BODY

If magick is a technology for manipulating psychic energy—treating it as a non-material stuff—how does this psychic stuff relate to the three-dimensions that material stuff occupies? I have already remarked upon the psychic characteristics of landscapes and power spots, and how we can split power off into talismans and then place them in proximity to the people we wish to influence, so I must presume that psychic energy has a relationship to physical space. But then where does it reside in our own bodies? Is it just some kind of fog that hovers around our brains and bellies in a non-specific way, or does it have an anatomy that relates directly to our physical anatomies, and which may affect the physical processes that take place within them–e.g. those necessary for physical health?

The sorcerer's answer to this is that we do have a psychic anatomy–called "the subtle body"–and that it is closely aligned to our central nervous systems, from the base of our spines up to the top of our brains. This anatomy has been recognized by eastern mystics for thousands of years; it has been incorporated during the past 130 years into the Western occult tradition; and it is beginning to be accepted by Western medicine, specifically in the form of acupuncture. Once we gain the ability to manipulate it, we can move psychic energy through our bodies at will. This is the only way to conjure with any sort of confidence, which makes mastery of the subtle body essential for full magickal development.

The foundation of this subtle anatomy is the central column that rises from the base of the spine to the top of the head. There are also branches out from it that run down the legs and along the arms, and the egg-shaped aura that encompasses the body as a whole.

The first step in the development of the subtle body is to make banishing a habit, since a well-defined aura is necessary to perceive power, to endure its presence, to accumulate it, and to hold it over time. The next step is the arousal and training of the Kundalini Serpent, which is the engine that drives the whole apparatus. Pictured as a snake that lies coiled at the base of the spine, it may be aroused through physical or emotional excitement, music and dance, acceleration (as on a motorcycle or roller coaster), controlled breathing, cannabis and psychedelic drugs, sexual activity, and physical and psychic manipulations during meditation.

Strung out along this central column are energy centers called chakras, each of which deals with energy in a different way. The number of chakras is a matter of some dispute. The Rosicrucians see five, the Tantric Buddhists six, the Tantric Hindus seven, and the Chinese Taoists about fifteen[7]. I've found a use for ten: 1.) the base of the spine, the source for Kundalini; 2.) the genitals, for splitting off energy so it has an independent identity; 3.) the belly, for storing power; 4.) the solar plexus, for sending power out; 5.) the heart, for emotional contact; 6.) the throat, for speech; 7.) the Third Eye, for vision; 8.) the hairline, as a source of power for sending out; 9.) the base of the skull, for protection ("eyes in the back of his head"); and 10.) the top of the head, our connection to the Highest.

[7] This would imply either 1) there is a definite number of chakras, and there is only one (at most) school that has it right; or 2) you get the subtle anatomy that you program onto yourself, and if you teach yourself (or allow someone to convince you) that there are five, then that's how many you'll get. In this view, the only real fact is the existence of the central column, and also that the energy goes up it when you inhale, and down when you exhale. It's also fairly safe to assume that the belly is the only place fit to store power.

The sorcerous approach to opening these up and using them is to treat each powerflow and each chakra as a separate spirit that may be met on the astral, named, and bound with a ritual charge. Then when you want to start the powerflow or open the chakra, you can call its name and it will become active. But then if you can open a chakra with a word, you need a word to close it as well. This, too, you may define on the astral, though a single word may suffice for them all.

To do a complete explanation of the astral mapping and manipulation of the subtle body is too complicated for this introduction. I offer a far more detailed look in the essays "The Subtle Body" and "Sending Power to Help and Hurt" in my *Taking Power*. For the present I would like to focus on three aspects of this work: 1.) activation of the subtle anatomy through circulation of the Light, 2.) the use of the belly chakra for the storage of energy, and 3.) self-healing.

1.) Circulation of the Light is a Taoist meditative practice whereby a person activates the Kundalini through breathing, visualization and muscular contractions, then uses it to drive a circulation of psychic energy throughout his or her body, even as the energy is kept well-confined within his or her aura. In the Chinese practice this is an elaborate discipline wherein the sage generates a mixture of sexual energy, vital force and aesthetic energy and uses it to spawn an immortal entity called "the crystal child." It requires a full assimilation of Chinese yoga and aesthetic culture. What I offer here is a much-simplified version, and if I do not promise immortality, I do suggest it as a way to produce greater physical integrity and more effective magick.

To begin this practice you should first sit down in your meditative posture and begin a steady breathing. The posture itself does not matter so long as your head is erect and your spine straight, nor need you be so concerned with immobility as you would during exercises of concentration. Once you are settled, you must arouse your Kundalini. To do this, tighten in quick succession the perineal muscles, the muscles right behind the anus, and the muscles in the lower back as you breathe in. Visualize the Snake as a Light rising in the spine, as if the contractions were drawing it on up. Then with the out breath relax and visualize the Light flowing back down.

This is the basic motion, but you might find that this movement of energy from the bottom up brings a corresponding flow from the top down–a flow that enters in through the top of the head on the in breath, and rushes up on out when you exhale. If you give these energy flows names and bind them as spirits, you can maintain the circulation just by chanting them as mantras.

Once the flows have been established, however, they need to be contained, lest they energize your environment as much as yourself. To do this, use them to form an egg of Light encompassing your head. On the inhalation, bring the Light up the spine, over the top of your head, down the front of your face, and tuck it under your chin to merge with the flow up the spine, thus forming the egg. At the same time, bring the Light from above in through the top of your head and down in front of your face to merge with the same ovoid. Then with the exhalation, let the energy run out.

You may find that the Light tends to form whorls on each side of the head. This energy must be drawn inwards to the point of view behind the eyes, rather than letting it flow outwards, where it might be lost. You should also define branching flows to include your arms and legs in the circulation–again, pushing the energy into them with the inhalation, letting it run out with the exhalation.

2.) Once you have carried out a circulation of your Light for more than a few minutes, your aura will be quite energized. When you decide to stop, the energy must be absorbed into your belly chakra, it being the only place where psychic energy may be stored safely. You can do this by imagining your belly as the hub of a wheel, with the spokes extending out from this center into your aura. Then imagine the wheel rotating and the spokes drawing the energy into this hub. You should keep at this until all feeling of excitement is gone and the belly is glowing with the energy thus captured. And again, if you give this process a name and bind it, you can work it simply by chanting the name as a mantra, even just whispering it to yourself.

The details here are important, but I can't really give them because, to my knowledge, they apply only to me. By details I mean things like which direction the wheel should rotate, whether it's a single wheel or a double wheel going opposite directions, the color of the Light, and so on. As we will see in Chapter 15, these details are indeed significant. So if you are going to do this work, you must develop competence at astral projection, because the astral plane is the place for learning things like this. You also need to become acquainted with your Holy Guardian Angel, who often enough will be able to answer such questions outright. With the Angel's assistance, you can begin to manipulate subtle mechanisms that do much to determine everything from charisma to physical health. This book here must only be seen as an introduction to what is possible. That is, I mean it to give you a notion of whether or not magick is something you wish to pursue. The book that you truly need here is one that you will write yourself–your own magickal record.

3.) A big reason to want to work with your subtle body is the health of your physical body. Not only does a habit of circulation of the Light lend a special harmony to its operation, but you can send energy out of your belly chakra to 'inspire' specific parts of yourself that seem to need it, often with strikingly good effect. Which is to say, you can use that energy to heal yourself of all sorts of ailments. You are, or at least should be, already in rapport with all aspects of your fleshy corpus; the feedback you get from putting energy into any part of it should be immediate and explicit. In fact, the simple effort of putting energy into it should tell you a great deal about what, if anything, is the matter.

I would note that such safety cannot be assumed when one attempts to heal others. Healing others is all well and good, and there is plenty of free power available if you're willing immediately to give it away, so it's not like you have to deplete yourself, but the need for a deep rapport with the patient is always a problem. If you don't have such a rapport, the energy can do more harm than good. If you do take care to develop it, your work can have much beneficial effect, but to put it bluntly, who wants to enter rapport with a bunch of sick people? Some of the sickness that's on them has to rub off, and no matter how well you clean yourself, it is very difficult to get it all. Over time it can accumulate to much bad effect. But if you don't attain the rapport, you won't get the feedback you need to know how the energy is working. You'll be just ramming power in instead of carefully readjusting it, which is about as effective as trying to rebuild a carburetor with a hammer and a screwdriver.

To use my energy to heal myself, then, my procedure is to cause the wheel centered in my belly to move in the direction opposite to that which I use to store power. I use my mind's eye to see the energy flowing out from my belly along the spokes, glowing blue-white, into the location of my ailment. For instance, for a respiratory infection it would fill the sinuses, throat and lungs; for a strained muscle or an injured knee, it would energize the muscle or joint itself. I will see the injury or infection within the location as either red or black, and fill it with energy until the red or black has been washed out and only the blue-white remains. The immediate result is that perhaps it will hurt a bit more than before, but this quickly passes and any improvements come soon after.

Two precautions are necessary here. Before beginning you must define your aura as a shell–either by banishing or else by chanting words that will define it as such–this to keep your energy from leaking out into space. And once you have finished, you should briefly, almost perfunctorily, wheel your energy back in, this to reabsorb any excess.

Finally, it is important to do this work immediately upon receiving an injury or perceiving a symptom of illness, since long-term afflictions take on lives of their own that can be difficult to extinguish. In fact, it is best to begin at once if you find you have been exposed to an infectious disease. As an example, I can recall a time when a close associate informed me she was coming down with a cold. Though I still felt perfectly healthy, I made several efforts to fill my sinuses and throat with Light. Within a day or two, the cold arrived, but its symptoms were essentially *compressed*, going through their usual sequence in only two days instead of ten. This for me was a nice confirmation of the efficacy of this practice. If I hadn't gotten sick at all, a skeptic could just say I already had an immunity or I just hadn't caught it. But to have it so briefly showed that something out of the ordinary intervened, and the magick would appear to be the most available explanation.

Chapter XIV
SEXUALITY

The genitals are the chakras for sending power out on its own and into the world. The essence of this energy is that it is creative of a new thing–a new human if nature takes its course, a new world if we have the ingenuity to put aside the natural and use the energy for what we can.

The connection between magick and sex is ancient and intrinsic, but hedged about with cautions and prohibitions, mostly because it is as effective as it is. Many of these cautions are a bit extreme, having more to do with social control than the management of psychic energy, but they all have an origin in the mechanics of its action, and so cannot be dismissed out of hand. The essential point is that the energy will create, in one way or another, and if it doesn't create a child, it will create something else. For the average man or woman, this might be only a slight creation, with minimal consequence, but this does not remain the case for those of us who set out to learn sorcery. As we gain power, and especially once we begin to use sex for magick, our spontaneous creations acquire consequence. If we don't claim control over our creative energies and cause them to make what we really want, they will fall under the influence of any passing psychic impetus, and oftentimes make nothing but problems. The obvious solution–technically known as "chastity"–is to be sure that whenever we emit such energy, we take the trouble to deal with it magickally. This might seem like a tall order, but as you begin to gain power, you will find it to be a necessity. Nor is the animation of psychic scavengers all that should concern us. As you gain power, it becomes as if it were more concentrated within you, so if you indulge in uncontrolled spending, it is a breach under pressure, which wastes more of it and robs what remains of the intensity it needs to accomplish your will.

The difference between men and women–in both anatomy and quality of energy–is conspicuous. Men eject the quickening jolt, the surge of power that animates the enterprise. Women provide the form that can thus be stirred to life. The fundamental strategy for working this magick is to prevent the energy from fulfilling its natural purpose–making babies–but this without allowing it to dissipate, and then to focus it into spawning the event you require. The vehicles for this energy that are the most potent and easiest to manipulate are semen and menstrual blood. The semen carries the energy. The blood is the living matrix frustrated of biological purpose, but still ready to accept whatever psychic form might be imposed upon it. You can impose this form through the use of traditional symbolism or with alphabetic sigils. The participants will visualize the meaningful glyph during the moment of orgasm; the combined fluids can then be used to consecrate a talisman decorated in the same manner. Thus the psychic energy is given the psychic imprint it needs to accomplish the given wish, to quicken its virtual form into an actual event. This event will be the meaningful coincidence that is the magickal result, often appearing as an unexpected opportunity. It must be immediately recognized as such and embraced so its special momentum may be applied to the situation before it dissipates back into the mundane.

The primary precautions that we must take here are banishing both before and after any operation, and chastity. Banishing is a necessity with any magickal operation, but all the more so when sexual energies are involved, since such rich food attracts more scavengers than leaner fare, spirits who would use it to advance their own agendas at the expense of our own. Chastity is an extension of this in that it stipulates that once one begins these practices, there must be no casual disposal of sexual fluids: semen, menstrual blood, or vaginal fluid–the elixirs, as they are called. All must be devoted to a purpose or, if this is not possible, then at least banished and thus kept from feeding random entities.

Scholars of the occult will find many precedents for this practice of chastity. Orthodox Jews require their women to attend ritual baths after their menstrual periods, and will not touch them until they have thus cleansed themselves. Sexual self-stimulation is condemned by religions both theistic and pagan. And homosexuality, even if not prohibited outright, is generally relegated to a social fringe, where it will tend not to corrupt the body politic.

For sorcerers such blanket prohibitions are only so much twaddle, similar to a tribe restricting metalwork to a special caste because metals are so dangerous. Yes, sexual fluids are potent to create, and if not dealt with carefully, will create in conformity with one's own worst tendencies. So, again, one must take care to ensure that whenever one has them they either create in accordance with will, or they create nothing at all. Some points:

1.) With sexual intercourse with a partner of the opposite sex, there is no magickal problem at all, regardless of whether or not children are a possible outcome. If contraception is used or there is some other cause for sterility, then the energy will go into building the relationship between the participants. The one caution here is against casual sex with whoever comes along, in that one will create chains of consequence connecting one with lots of people one may not wish to be connected with in the long run. Of course Aleister Crowley was one of the most promiscuous men alive, and yet never seemed inconvenienced by such entanglements. *But then he did take care to treat each sexual liaison as a magickal act*, dedicating the energy to some purpose or another and using the fluids to either charge a talisman or consuming them as a Eucharist.

2.) Sexual self-stimulation may be treated in the same way. Simply put, always have a purpose in mind and a sigil or symbol available to concentrate upon during the moment of orgasm. Then either use the fluids produced as a Eucharist, or to consecrate a talisman. When consuming it as a Eucharist, you should hold the elixir in your mouth and visualize it as glowing with Light. Then open your belly chakra and begin to wheel it in for storage, the spokes of the wheel grabbing the Light as they pass through your mouth and drawing it into the hub behind your naval. Then when the Light in your mouth has dimmed, go ahead and swallow.

With talismans, it helps if they are hollow, so as to be able to contain what you want to put in them. Once charged, talismans are often wrapped up and put away, with the magician only unwrapping and carrying them when he wants to have their particular power. Or if you want to spawn a specific type of event, talismans may be planted. The English occultist Kenneth Grant suggests burying a talisman meant to cause a material effect, hanging from a tree those meant to bring information, submerging in fresh water those intended to have an emotional or sexual effect (attracting partners, etc.), and burning talismans intended to have a creative effect. All in all, this sort of magick takes a lot more trouble than the simple consumption of a Eucharist. With the talisman, care must be taken to provide an artificial matrix for the energy to activate; for instance, the magician could draw his sigil in his own blood, then place it in the container he will fill with semen. With the Eucharist, your matrix is your own body, and you absorb the energy to move your life as a whole in the direction you want it to go. Thus I suspect that for the frequent usage required by a young sorcerer brimming with more semen than he can stand, the Eucharistic option will be more palatable.

3.) According to Aleister Crowley, menstrual blood is most useful on the second day of its flow–diminishing in potency after that, but on the first day too dangerous for use. I would remark that through the use of menstrual blood, heterosexual potencies can be applied to solitary working. With none of the usual distractions, all of the male energy produced, along with all his semen, could go into the talisman, and a sigil drawn in the woman's blood would form a more potent matrix for that energy than could be created with the man's own. Even if a couple slept together every night, they could find advantages to doing results magick in this way–keeping the money magick out of the bedroom, so to speak.

4.) Homosexual sex magick is something I have never tried, but according to Crowley (who did a lot of it) the dynamic is fundamentally different. As he summed it up in his *Liber Aleph*, opposites tend to produce a stable "child" which is resistant to change, but those who are alike "increase mutually the potential of their particular natures." Which is to say, men and women unite to form a new thing with an identity and hence a karma of its own, while partners of the same sex repel, each sending the other more swiftly in his or her destined direction. This would do much to explain both the creativity gays tend to display in the arts, and also the fact that frequent partner exchange is an accepted aspect of the gay lifestyle.

Now I must emphasize in all these remarks that I am limited to the particular perspective of a heterosexual male. I know the energetic qualities of semen from my own experience, but those of vaginal fluid are something of a mystery. Also, since the energies of male orgasm are so thoroughly embodied in semen, I can't say I've looked into orgasm's more aetherial energies, which for a woman could be the most important of all. And of course I haven't a clue about the psychic characteristics of menstrual blood as encountered on a monthly basis. These are not things that are available to me, and I cannot rely on my own logic to tell me what I have no way of feeling first hand. If my reticence presents a problem, all I can say is ***Do your own research!***

Chapter XV
DOING YOUR OWN RESEARCH

When we think of doing research, we can tend to think of science. Of course magick is not scientific. This is a fact that the scientists can seem anxious to assert, as if it meant that magick were not real, and all the effort spent on trying to cause change magickally is wasted. But this is only bluster. Just because the scientific method is incompetent to address psychic energy, that doesn't mean psychic energy cannot spawn human event, which is mostly the result of psychic action anyway. It just means the scientific method will not be the epistemological tool to use with magick once we figure out all the details of working it.

The scientific method is incapable of dealing with psychic energy because psychic energy cannot be made into an object to be studied. Science demands the capacity to measure phenomena and reproduce them, but there is no way to calibrate psychic energy except our own feel for it, and each sorcerer's purpose, circumstances and state of mind–the apparatus and conditions for the experiment–will be unique. Though the whole point of science is its embrace of "objectivity," psychic energy defies this standard by its very being[8]. An observer can't even observe it without being compromised by it. The energy we manipulate to do magick is the same energy we use to manage the manipulations, and also the same energy we use to perceive the results of our efforts. We can only judge its potency through the intensity it displays in our own psyches, and even here we must wonder if that might be a function of how susceptible we are to it, as when a power spot seems more potent when we have depleted our own reserves through heavy use. In the end, magick will always be more an art than a science.

But just because the nature of psychic energy defies scientific analysis, that doesn't mean those of us who would exploit it can't take a scientific attitude. There are lots of things that scientists do when they do science that can help a sorcerer do magick.

One thing that scientists do that sorcerers absolutely must do is keep accurate records. Your subtle

[8] Which may be why so many scientists would say it can't exist.

and astral work, the sigils you draw and the spirits you bind, the behavior of an elemental and the results of a conjuration–you will remember all these more clearly if you put them down on paper. Blood on parchment is not required. A spiral notebook and a cheap ballpoint will suffice. But just do it.

Another point is the need to practice the exercises until you are easy with them. Competence in astral projection and a well-defined subtle body are not the results of magickal work, but the tools for doing it, and if you are not fluid in their movements, you will not be quick enough to respond to the fluid ways power will lead you. I have offered exercises that will encourage the development of this quickness, these in chapters on banishing, yoga, the subtle body and sexuality, and I have described what is involved with astral projection and the Holy Guardian Angel. With all these we can increase our ability to perceive, manage and respond to psychic energy, to generate it, store it and apply it to our circumstances to cause change. You must be able to recognize powerflow and respond to it reflexively, as you would to a ball when catching it and throwing it back.

As an example from my own progress, I can recall that several weeks after I took on the discipline of chastity, my silver ring began to turn black. This seemed curious, but it was a hot summer, I was swimming in salt water, and I felt fine. But then there came a day when I had an elixir in mouth, getting set to wheel it into my belly chakra, and I felt the absolute necessity of having the wheel turn in the opposite direction. It was simply the way it went now. And within a week the ring, once polished, stayed white again, even as it was still hot and I was still swimming in salt water.

The unavoidable implication is that by taking on the discipline of chastity, I created a subtle malfunction that displayed itself through the production of corrosive sweat, and that with the subtle correction, the display ceased. One wonders, then, what the effect might have been if I had not developed the ability to engage my subtle body before I took on this discipline. Would I have done some real damage? Of course it's possible that if I had not previously defined the motion the belly chakra uses to absorb energy, it would have adjusted itself without my being aware of it. But then if I hadn't defined it, what tool would I have been using all along to absorb the elixir's power before swallowing it, which is surely the best way to do it? How, indeed, would I even know that such a deliberate storage was possible? It is possible that by taking on the discipline of subtle body manipulation, all that I have really done is imposed a pattern of energy movement onto myself that otherwise would not be there. But then does this matter, so long as through this imposed pattern I am able to move energy to promote my will?

I call this chapter "Doing Your Own Research," but the process I describe here involves much more than just discovering knowledge. You are building a tool–your own Self–fit to handle power, and it is needful that you take your time so it has a chance to properly cure, lest it break *in extremis*. This is to say, magickal power must be pursued in stages. Magick must be a lifetime sort of thing, so it certainly makes sense to spend a few years gaining skill in the easier disciplines (making banishing a habit, yoga, "Liber III") before beginning subtle body work and astral projection. And then it's best to get a good feel for these before you start to move any substantial energy around, for instance with sex magick. And it is only when you are dealing with these more potent forces that disciplines like chastity are unavoidable.

So chastity is essential if you are using sexual energies for magick. But even if you are restricting yourself to more subtle methods, you may reach a point when the need for it will be obvious, and your astral advisors and oracles will let you know if you are too dense to figure it out for yourself. This is in fact what happened to me. When my Holy Guardian Angel told me I needed it (not a surprise), I wasn't using sexual energies in magick. But I was working through a series of exercises in rising on the planes wherein I had discovered some elaborate astral architectures that carried subtle connections and allowed for movement between these "planes." Also, I was regularly drinking water from a power spot as an elixir and experimenting with other sacraments of notorious potency. So it wasn't as if I wasn't pushing it, and by pushing it I made it necessary to add the discipline of chastity, and perforce the practice of sex magick, to my ongoing magickal repertoire.

My mention of astral architectures established through the practice of rising on the planes brings us to another problem–astral veracity.

Rising on the planes is the practice of stepping onto the astral and simply willing oneself to rise, then taking account of all the edifices, orifices, entities and landscapes that one encounters on the way up. For those who have assimilated a Rosicrucian system, for instance that of Aleister Crowley, what one sees will all be organized in terms of the Tree of Life of the Hermetic Qabalah–with the planes arranged in terms of the four worlds and the ten Sephiroth connected by the 22 paths, each location with its own set of characteristic symbols and inhabited by characteristic gods and devils, angels and demons, who may grant knowledge and power to those who enter into a relationship with them. Using my own freeform approach and the guidance of my Holy Guardian Angel, what I discovered was the passageway between the planes, their inhabitants, and the conduits through which my chakras connect to all levels. But however you decide to organize what you find there, if you work on yourself in terms of that understanding, you will be rewarded with all sorts of insights on how to better integrate magick into your life as a whole. Psychic energy will become a palpable thing and magick realized as the technology for manipulating it.

But though experience will show magick to be real enough as a method for moving psychic energy, what about the symbolic architectures and maps of power–and the individual spirits who claim to act with power–that we meet in the course of using it? The effects we produce when we conjure are real enough, but what about the gods we invoke to bring us the power we need to do it? Are they intelligences with their own independence, or are they simply personalities out of our own unconscious that we project upon power in order to interact with it? And what of the efficacy of the pentagrams and hexagrams that Rosicrucian magicians use to banish the demons and conjure the planetary powers? Is there something special about those shapes, or is the fact that they're traditional sufficient to produce the effect?

In short, do I have any right to claim that the entities I deal with when I manipulate psyche to do magick have any reality outside my own head? Enough reality, perhaps, that other people should learn all about them while I elaborate their astral apparitions with architectures of dogma, and canons of morality–so all will have the opportunity to draw power from these deities I have discovered?

Of course if everyone who adheres to this revealed Truth actually can draw power from it, or if a large enough percentage can, then is a religion born, and all is lost.

Both Austin Spare and Aleister Crowley rejected this notion of true symbolism. Austin Spare wrote, "The beliefs we make are the best for us, whatever their truth. Any belief is sanctified by the believing, and justified by results."[9] And as Crowley wrote at the beginning of his "Liber O," concerning the Gods, Spirits, Sephiroth, Planes and other symbolic entities described there:

> *It is immaterial whether they exist or not. By doing certain things certain results follow; students are most earnestly warned against attributing objective reality or philosophical validity to any of them.*

Crowley's "Liber O" is a manual on how to do astral projection and ceremonial conjuring in terms of Rosicrucian symbolism. The results from using these methods can be real enough, but what of the entities in whose terms the techniques operate? How real are they? Not real at all, is Crowley's answer. They are only effective.

Perhaps the best way to look at these magickal entities–astral architectures and landscapes, symbols,

[9] From "The Logomachy of Zos," published in Kenneth and Steffi Grant's *Zos Speaks!*, p. 175.

gods, and spirits–is as tools. They are made entirely of psychic stuff and the astral will generate them spontaneously to accommodate whatever symbolic scheme you would project upon it. As psychic stuff they are fit to manipulate psychic energy. It is for this purpose that ceremonial magicians assimilate them so they might have a terminology with which to focus their energy and call it up. Since we can spawn them or discard them at will, the question of how *true* they are seems somewhat moot. The values by which to judge them are effectiveness, ease of use, and relevance to the task at hand. Can they do the job of magick well and with a minimum of fuss? And does the specific job they were designed to do still need doing at all?

Taking my own experience as an example, you will recall that I began this discussion with references to the astral architectures I had developed in the process of rising on the planes. In point of fact, I had simply gone up accompanied by my Angel and with her assistance named and bound the locations and structures that I discovered as I did so, and also the entities that inhabited them. Since my inclination at the time was to assume that something called "the Absolute"[10] was at the origin of individual consciousness, my edifice tended to reach toward something that felt like it could be that. Also, I worked to make definite connections between the chakras operating in my fleshy self and this more aetherial source of energy. And in the course of doing all this I was told that I had reached the point where the discipline of chastity was a necessity. So I took that discipline on. And then my ring turned black. I fixed that, and then I learned a lot of other stuff, too, for instance how to best confine my power during circulations of the Light, about the technique of synthesizing spirits to render usable energy out of negative inclinations, and why vampirism is a self-defeating way to accumulate energy–more a vice than a strategy.

In their way, all of these were a consequence of my taking the trouble to define my astral architecture and hook up my energy flow in its terms. But even though the technical innovations thus spawned serve me well to this day, for the life of me I hardly remembered the architecture itself until I started looking through my magickal record so I could write the bit about the ring turning black. I didn't

[10] The undifferentiated origin of all manifestation, also known as "Tao" or the Neoplatonic "One."

remember the names of the places or the character of the guardians, just a vague image of the topology of the place. Of course it's all written down in my magickal record, so I could reconstruct it if I wanted to, though whether it would have any relevance to my current psychic geometry is anybody's guess. At this point, one could see it as a disused scaffold, pushed away from my finished edifice of magickal practice to be covered with greenbrier and wild roses, and certainly not likely to get in the way of any new scaffolding to be assembled for future installations. By giving it no claim to truth in the first place, it never had any hope of reality, so it's easy to let it slide when it's time to move on.

On the other hand, I did not take it down, nor would I think it wise to do so now. After all, I did make a number of subtle connections through it, so just cleaning it all out could be like digging up your front yard and cutting your gas and water lines. And anyway, I didn't define this astral topology out of my conscious will (in which case I should have reabsorbed it), but simply discovered it and integrated it into my magickal universe. But even if it does have an "independent" reality in my psychic make-up, I would never suggest that anyone else's should follow my pattern, and I would emphasize that my discovery of my own was more valuable to me from the effort of making it than from any "Great Psychic Truths" thus revealed. So again: *Do your own research!*

Such is the way of magick, which takes its tolerance from traditional paganism, which was always ready to accept another man's way of accessing power. The opposite path, of course, is that of Theistic religions, which believe there is only One True Way to organize and understand the power we deal with, and they know what it is. And because they know the Source of All Grace, if you disagree, you must be divorced from the Source of All Grace, and thus evil, and thus damned to hell. Such lines of thought become inevitable when we invest our magickal tools with belief, and worship them, for then we displace our ends with our means, and give over our wills to an abstraction. It is a turning away from all that is magickal within us, abandoning all power to some Great Holy Other so we might be spared the trouble of learning how to deal with it ourselves.

Chapter XVI
CONJURE WITHOUT CEASING!

Magick is only effective to the extent you use it. Regardless of our knowledge, we must make it part of momentary awareness if it is to matter at all. If we do not, magick will at best be a hobby, at worst an affectation. We must do the disciplines–frequent banishing for the rest of our lives, exercises of will like that given by *Liber III vel Jugorem*, and the definition and exercise of power flows in the subtle body–but these will have only an indirect effect on how we live our lives, providing occult options and the power to exercise them, but no impetus for doing so. To live magickally requires an ongoing awareness of the power all around us and how our own power interacts with it. If we aren't aware of these powerflows, we cannot correct inefficiencies in our use of them, nor can we manipulate them for any specific end.

One way to become aware of power is to deliberately turn our attentions to it, but that's sort of what I've been talking about throughout this book–the techniques given, if actually used, tending to do this. Another approach would be to address the habits of thought that actively hide power from us, and use magick to counter these. And this shall be our concern in this penultimate chapter.

Just by being alive, we produce an ongoing quantity of psychic energy. We can use it to contrive and carry out actions in the world, we can conjure with it, we can give and receive it in emotional interplay with other people, we can store it. Or we can waste it building and maintaining a fantastic interpretation of the world with little bearing on reality past, present or future. And though the productive uses are what make our lives, so much energy is squandered in these fantasies, and so much attention misdirected, if we could correct it, we would do much to enable our lives to become magickal. This is because these fantasy worlds don't simply waste power, they conceal it. They take us out of the present and place us in past or future, and we can only find power right here, now.

There are two steps to resolving this issue: 1.) determining which thought-streams promote productive work and which are emotional self-indulgence, and 2.) redirecting the energy that animates the self-indulgence into something useful. The solution to the first is a sort of philosophical touchstone, the second a stratagem of sorcery.

1.) The philosophical touchstone relies on Austin Spare's dual principle, recounted in Chapter VII, that there is no truth anywhere that is not balanced by an equally true opposite somewhere. In Aleister Crowley's formulation, the rubric for it is $0=2$. $0 \neq 1$. There is no creation out of nothing. But $0=(+1)+(-1)$, creation into balanced opposites that rarely if ever recombine. This principle pervades physical science. Matter is opposed by antimatter. Momentum counters gravity. The mutual dance of positive and negative electrical charge results in all the chemical complexity of the universe and the life in it. Energy demands entropy. There is no action without an equal and opposite reaction.

What this means in practice is that if you happen upon one extreme, you must always look for its opposite and incorporate that into your understanding of the situation, or you will base your enterprise on an error. And this applies to psychic enterprises as well as physical ones. You can't get something for nothing. Excessive enforcement conjures rebellion. Obsessive love conjures resentment. There is no desire without the possibility of satiety. There is no action without an equal and opposite reaction. And 0=2 applies to *everything*. Thus if a vivid thought cannot incorporate such an opposite, we may presume that we have an emotional bias towards this thought–that is important to us emotionally that it be *true*–a bias which will produce error if left uncorrected. But if we can find the opposite and juxtapose it to it, that emotional energy will be released in an act of Neither-Neither, the resulting free belief made available for magick.

The assiduous application of 0=2–making it a standard against which any thought is habitually held—is an essential achievement for those who would pursue competence in sorcery. Not only does its guidance help preclude honest error and miscalculation, immunize us from political and religious extremes of every variety, and enable energy release through the Neither-Neither, but it is an efficient counter to any sort of obsessive thought-stream, able to indicate all the curtains that keep us from seeing power. Which is to say...

2.) We meet power in the immediate present. It can't be in the future, because the future hasn't happened yet, and the past provides only precedent and momentum. So we will not find it in nostalgia for the past or expectations of the future. We may take guidance from the past and must prepare for the future, but these are specific acts in the present–the hunt of the scholar, the open-minded recollection of significant events, the work to lay up goods before winter or prepare defense against possible aggression–and have nothing to do with our moment-to-moment mental contents when we are not thus engaged. Of course we might excuse ourselves when we are in the grip of obsession by claiming that we are considering likely contingencies for the future, or consequences from the past, but an application of 0=2 will generally give the lie to that. It will demonstrate that our presumed future is dominated by emotional bias, one way or another, and our dwelling on the past only wastes our psychic energy in a futile attempt to "make it all better now." In the process these hide the ongoing play of power between ourselves and the world. The alternatives here are that we either extract power from them to do our wills, or we wallow in delusion.[11]

The first step to disposing of these fantasy worlds is to understand what sort of desire they would bring to satiety. They certainly don't accomplish anything except to produce an emotional excitation, one way or another: exaltation or despair. In general it would seem that they seek to satisfy the unsatisfiable–to make right in mind some trauma, deprivation, rage, anxiety, or deep emotional need that is otherwise beyond reach, either because it is in the past or because to realize it in the future would violate the laws of man, God

[11] One may reply that with the invention of the smartphone, one is no longer restricted to either productive awareness or delusion, but can blot out one's obsessive thought with YouTube videos, news website updates, social media, and streaming movies. But this is an escape from obsession, not mastery over it, a way to shirk responsibility for one's own consciousness, a sort of cyber-opium that anesthetizes any disturbing aspects of Self with dead text. The web offers wonderful tools. I personally am a frequent user of Wikipedia, and if there's nothing on the radio when I'm working, I can always call up Miles Davis on YouTube and let him play while I'm writing on Word. And email is essential. But I don't carry it around with me all the time, and one of Miles' particular benefits is that his art leaves plenty of room for my own thought. Music can serve as thought's soundtrack, and power's, too, enhancing it rather than effacing it, and when you're sitting closed up in a box anyway, why not?

or physics. In my own case, a dominant theme has been anger at the civil state. When I first discerned that my fulminations against it were an energy-wasting indulgence rather than a justified condemnation of an awful reality, I tried to treat this tendency as a demon, evoke it, and bind it into silence. This approach had worked fine with some of my more personal foibles–the expectation of conflict in the case of any interpersonal interaction, for instance–but my magickal efforts against anger at the State failed, simply because the rage was too justified by bitter experience, the historical record, and the State's ongoing cupidities and arrogations. Reveling in its sovereign immunity and its license to kill, its minions all too often arrogant, self-serving and stupid, capable of ruining the lives of whomever it touches–and with the cyber revolution, now capable of touching everyone, all the time–simple justice cries out for its annihilation.

An application of 0=2 makes clear the absurdity of such a program. An honest look at human nature reveals that without the State's hard hand, life truly would be "solitary, poor, nasty, brutish and short." And I must admit that for me to carry out of my fantasies of retribution would lead to my own destruction, simply because they tend to be so over the top that they would of necessity conjure inescapable retribution, hubris bringing nemesis being as certain a progression as energy ending in entropy. So there can be no point, and an ongoing anger at the State can only be a waste of energy and a veil over the play of power going on around me each instant.

But as said, I could not successfully bind it; it was too deeply rooted in my personality for me to just yank it out, and so was its voice as persistent as ever. But then I got the flash that I should not address the spirit that generated the anger, but the energy of the anger itself. That is, I should not try to prevent or control the voice's appearance, but whenever it did appear, I needed a way to convert that anger–which is only psychic energy animating that particular template of meaning–into something productive. To eliminate a thought, a trick of thought is needed, and for a sorcerer this can be a spirit specifically synthesized to deal with the problem. And so with my Holy Guardian Angel's help I conjured, named and bound the spirit that transforms anger at the civil state into literary creativity. With this the energy is not stifled, as it would be if I could treat it as a demon to be compelled to silence, but rerouted into something useful. Literary creativity is certainly that, and it is a purpose that does not contradict rage against the State. Since the preeminence of the individual as an Eye of God is a subtext in my sorcerous writing, it would seem that my work to describe and publish the art must support opposition to it, since the best way to smash the State is to encourage a type of human who doesn't need it, and has the power to be shut of it. And so now whenever some news item, government edict, or random recollection sparks a rant, all I have to do is speak the name and the rant shortly ends. What once occupied a half an hour now can be dismissed in seconds, its energy presumably going into my powers of literary expression. I'm in no position to judge that, but the rant does stop.

Of course one must actually call the spirit for this to happen. If the fantasy itself provides enjoyment, one may perhaps not get around to speaking the name, and it will continue spinning its impossibilities in its most pathological way. Nor does a mere rote recitation of the name really work.

To make the anger gone one must call the spirit with full intent. It doesn't have to be any sort of ritual, but when you make the call, it does require concentration on that act. That doesn't mean I must then like the State, only that I would have the spirit drain the power from the particular denunciation going on right now so its passionate intensity goes away and doesn't bother me. And maybe the power animating it will go into something I can use.

Theoretically, this approach can be applied to any sort of habitual thought-stream, though I must admit my experience is limited by my own tendency of thought. That is, my habitual rants are active, aggressive, even belligerent, never passive or melancholic, and those who suffer from melancholia may encounter issues with this technique beyond my poor experience. But whether the energy is devoted to a denunciation of an external oppressor or a laceration of one's own Self, energy it remains and if we have the courage to address it, sorcery provides the technique to transform it for use it to a better end.

But one common thread stands out–all such obsessive thought takes us out of the present, spawning worlds of either retrospection or anticipation, but always effacing now, which is where the power is. Rehashing past weakness and incapacity, or picturing scenes of triumph to come, obviously does this, but so does worry, lust, greed, even contentment. All shift attention from the immediate world of matter and power to a speculative world where trouble is eternal, ecstasy is assured, wealth secured, or satiety given duration. Personally I find retrospection to be unsatisfying, so my own fantasies tend more toward anticipation; if I recall a past injustice, it will immediately evoke thoughts of future retribution, and "what I *should* have done" never enters into it. And so I have also found it useful to synthesize the spirit that transforms the energy animating anticipation into personal power. It is a broad-spectrum synth which, if called, will render any anticipation–from literary success or perfect anarchy to the attainment of true love or a trip to the dentist–into a generalized energy which I can then store (by wheeling it into my belly chakra) or use for conjuration (by visualizing a sigil). Of course if the rant involves anticipations of what would happen if I won power over the State, I would certainly employ both synthetic spirits against it.

To close, all I can do is stress that each personality is unique, and the specific way yours uses power is something for you to determine. Fear is failure, ensures failure, and no coward has the virtue to carry out this work with success. Magick is indeed dangerous simply because it is effective, and all things that are effective are dangerous if misapplied. But you'll never know how to apply it correctly if you don't start. "The occult secrets may not be taught, but may be learned." Solve it as you go along!

Chapter XVII
MAGICKAL POLITICS

Psychic energy is a substance that magicians intentionally manipulate to cause events and obtain insights that promote their wills. All aspects of magick either involve such manipulations or else consist of disciplines that train us to better manage and endure the presence of psychic energy–whether it is inside us or in the outside world. Magick distinguishes itself from religion by insisting that it is the technique for moving the energy that matters, not the dogmas that in one way or another attempt to somehow guarantee a safe supply. Which is to say, magick holds that psychic energy is morally neutral. It is how we apply it–and what sort of spirits and demons we call up when we do so–that produces the ethical consequences for both magicians and religionists alike. But power is power, and if we know what we are doing we can get it from dancing to a good technobeat as well as with celibacy, fasting, and devotion to the Virgin. From this it must follow that competence as a magician is more important for getting "God on our side" than allegiance to a particular belief system and the social structure it supports.

Put simply, magicians do not rest well under the broad wing of authority. A magician's awareness of the power flow that animates a situation will be deeper and more immediate, but with a broader perspective, than that of any "supervising authority" that might attempt to impose its will upon him–whether this be an individual human, a bureaucracy, or a social code. This does not mean such authority is always wrong, and when it is justified (e.g. traffic laws), it is certainly best to go with the flow. But any fundamental submission to it limits and distorts our access to power, and cripples our use of it. Expedience and subtlety justify the appearance of conformity to authority, but belief in its right to run things contradicts the intrinsic divinity of the individual. To actualize this divinity we must understand that it has its own momentum within each person, and we must discover and encourage this momentum if the divinity is to act to empower our lives.

Summarized as a social code for sorcerers, this can be most easily stated as "Do what thou wilt shall be the whole of the Law."

This admonition is very well known among magicians in the West, it being the prime imperative of *Liber AL vel Legis*–"The Book of the Law." This is a short text that the English magician Aleister Crowley transcribed in Cairo in 1904, writing from the dictation of a disembodied voice that called itself Aiwass, "the minister of Hoor-paar-kraat."

Here the symbolism gets a bit complicated. Hoor-paar-kraat is an aspect of the Egyptian falcon-god Horus. Horus has dozens of forms, all with hawk's heads, but in the singular case of Hoor-paar-kraat the form is no falcon, but a human infant with his finger to his lips in a gesture of Silence. Hoor-paar-kraat is paired in the Book with a contrary aspect of Horus, Ra-Hoor-Khuit, who is very much a falcon and the personification of the sun in its greatest heat. In the symbolism of the Book they represent the passive and the active aspects of psychic energy. Through our experience of psychic energy we learn how it manufactures reality, how we can use it to do the same, and what we must do with ourselves to do that safely. It is time for us humans to master this power that animates our own consciousness, before we destroy ourselves with our rage and our technics. The law given in *Liber AL vel Legis* permits and encourages this mastery, insisting only that we take control over our own power and use it to take pleasure in existence.

The Book of the Law comes in three chapters. The declaration of Ra-Hoor-Khuit takes up the last (Hoor-paar-kraat naturally does not speak), while the first two are the statements of Nuit and Hadit, the parents of Horus according to the Book's cosmology. Together with him they provide a scheme for creation that justifies the law the Book declares. Nuit is Infinite Space, everything we can experience. Hadit is the infinitesimal point of view, what there is inside us that is ultimately conscious. Nuit is female, Hadit is male, and their intercourse produces a child–psychic energy–that defines the Universe.

Liber Legis offers "Do what thou wilt" as a social code for the next several thousand years. "Do what thou wilt" is not "do what you please;" will is far deeper than whim. Nuit tells us that she is

"Infinite Space and the Infinite Stars thereof," and that "every man and every woman is a star." Thus the model for social order is that of stars in a galaxy. Each orb has its own momentum and proper motion that it simply falls into. There are no stellar supervisors or galactic governments to tell the individual orbs how to move. Crowley tells us that the only possible error is collision, or as the Book puts it, "The Word of Sin is Restriction."

In the end, what the Book presents is a hedonistic pantheism. Everything is god, and All Things exist so god can take pleasure in the interaction. We are eyes of god, along with every cat and rat and frog and fly, and together we supply god with infinite entertainment. "I am divided for love's sake," Nuit tells us, "for the chance of union." Thus as one might expect, the sacrament for Nuit is physical love. "Love is the law, love under will." If we are doing our wills when we encounter love, and if this love empowers our progress instead of distracting us from it, it doesn't matter how or with whom we go about it, so long as the prohibition against restriction is respected. In this way the engine for creation is made available to each individual so he or she might create the world that he or she desires. Whether the product of the intercourse is children or power or simply ecstasy is up to the individual–nothing that concerns any State or Church or any other authority in heaven or upon the earth or under the earth.

Thou art God!

Afterword
for the Second Edition

REGARDING THE GREATER STRUGGLE

1. Constriction

In the Introduction I warned of "the senescence of empire" assimilating the entire earth, "leaving no place anyplace as a refuge from its inevitable collapse." In the six years since, the cracks in this imperial edifice have become more widespread, revealing economic as well as geopolitical frailties that bode ill for its long-term vigor and even its survival. For anyone who feels oppressed by this hegemony, this decrepitude might seem like a good thing, but it doesn't necessarily help us. The system still retains its material vigor, and its efforts to save itself may have deep and debilitating effects upon the human race as such before these efforts' futility is finally acknowledged. Alternatives must be found, in one way or another, if chaos, extinction, or a Borg-like transformation into mindless social-insect-like hominids is to be avoided.

The psychic technology I have offered in this book is one such alternative. In this *Afterword* I hope to make its necessity explicit.

When I wrote the Introduction back in 2004, my attention had been drawn to the United States' intervention in Iraq. My fear was that by invading Iraq we had made inevitable its eventual fragmentation, to be followed by a hundred years war in the heart of Petrolstan as these fragments–Shiite, Sunni and Kurdish–sorted things out between themselves and their neighbors. This concern has not in any way diminished, even as our withdrawal goes on apace under the direction of the Obama administration, because sectarian violence is returning as American troops are leaving and the Iraqi government seems incapable of dealing with it. But the United States needs the forces it is withdrawing to hold Afghanistan, that strange realm that Alexander couldn't hold, the Mongols couldn't hold, the British couldn't hold, and the Russians couldn't hold. So, no, none of those fractures have in any way been mended, and it remains as likely as ever that the whole thing–oil included–could ultimately devolve into a chaos of blood and fire.

But as we all know, in the five years since *Shaping Formless Fire* first appeared there has been another cascade of events calling into doubt the solidity of the Grand Edifice–the housing bubble and the world-wide financial readjustment caused by its bursting. Anyone who has followed it will have heard many reasons for its occurrence: money lent to unqualified borrowers, money conjured up through bizarre, entirely unregulated financial instruments, interest rates kept low enough to fuel these reckless endeavors with borrowed money that the taxpayers are now responsible for, even as the bankers get to keep their outlandish bonuses. But knowing the fault says nothing about the ability of the Status Quo to repair it. After all, the business of America is business, and money needed to be lent so developers could develop, and securities needed to be packaged so that money could be lent, and interest rates had to be kept low to preserve full-employment, without which the trickle-down of wealth from the corporate masters to the mass of humanity would cease, leaving chaos and class war as the inescapable end. So none of the weaknesses are avoidable, but must be adjusted to. The financial system must be perfectly "tuned" to allow for a sufficient level of stimulation without boiling over into asset bubbles whose bursting will require repeated state intervention at the price of ever more onerous public debt.

It would seem that the whole economic system must become like the patient with the mild case of bipolar disorder who takes just enough medication to stay pleasantly manic–always on the up-swing, never so high that he makes the crash inevitable. But this can only be done when the disorder is stable. If the condition fluctuates, such fine adjustment is impossible, and ultimately the patient will spiral out of control, pulling those imprudent enough to be in rapport with him into the pit after him.

But the patient isn't stable, and the State is so involved in the corporate order that the doom of one must bring that of the other. And the instability comes from so many different directions. There is the aforementioned disintegration in Petrolstan, making the energy situation uncertain indeed, and there is also the spread of productive capacity across the developing world. Education and communications technology have enabled the creation of a global economy capable of producing wealth for all, if only it can obtain sufficient resources to build the productive capacity necessary to do it. Since some of those resources are of limited supply–energy and metals, for the most part–this unmeetable demand stimulated with easy money must create asset bubbles as a matter of course, surely too many for the Masters of Finance to regulate them all, or not without causing novel catastrophes in unanticipatable ways, yet still (in hindsight) consistent with the chaotic complexity of the economic system as a whole.

Of course the apologists for the system will insist there is a solution to this conundrum: more and better technology. Cheaper solar cells will solve the problem of energy; carbon fiber will replace aluminum; ever more pervasive computer controls will regulate the flow of everything to attain optimum efficiency, and hence minimal waste. Ultimately Petrolstan will be able, if it so chooses, to collapse into total chaos and the world will need only look on in exasperated despair, without any panic over economic ramifications.

The trouble is that more and better technology means more and better productive capacity, which means more and stronger demand for those scarce resources needed where there is no technological fix. When cheap solar cells are perfected, the most remote indigenous populations will have electricity to power their unique manufactories, producing product for which there will be a real demand. This demand will satisfy itself by inspiring the manufacture of machines, roads, vehicles, fuel–using up more resources in the process. And so they will grow scarce, regardless of the extent that their use in any particular product has been diminished through technological innovation. That is, for the foreseeable future machines will be made out of steel, and concrete reinforced with it. The use of electricity will still require copper, both to transmit it and in coils to make motors. Asphalt will still be compounded out of petroleum, and vehicles will largely be fueled by the stuff. Or if electric vehicles are perfected, their batteries will require all sorts of exotic metals, so esoteric will be the optimum technology. So there will be ever more pressure to develop further technological solutions, with the implied requirement that society–and through it, our own human nature–conform to whatever structural adjustments the solutions make necessary.

But there might also be a more fundamental problem with the system's faith in technology, deeper than the immediate difficulty of demand and supply, something for which depletion of resources and financial instability are mere symptoms. What if more and better technology can only be a temporary fix, not only incapable of getting us over the hump, but leading us deeper into the pit? This might seem counterintuitive at first. After all, how can making matter serve us better be a bad thing? But what if it does nothing to move us toward the direction that we need to be headed, but only to a point of diminishing returns? Reliance on the true promise that technology once did have could now be bringing back the peril it helped us escape from in the first place, which it is incapable of resisting any longer, but now can only advance.

Which is to say, ***incoherence.***

2. Decrepitude

Consider the possibility that even the most fantastic technical innovations cannot stave off a collapse once a culture grows too far past its maturity, just as the most expensive medical technology cannot keep the elderly billionaire alive forever.

This might seem an odd circumstance to bring up in this brave new world of hyper-technology, mastery of matter and reaching for the outer planets and all, but anyone with an eye to history will know that the quest that won this mastery has dominated the Western mind for centuries. From the Crusades to the European colonization of the world to the journeys to the moon and planets, the whole impetus of the West has been to ensure that there is no place anyplace not under its control–and producing profit–with our perfection of technology as the means to get us there. And even if the façade that we see all around us is shiny and new and never before seen on the face of the earth, that does not mean that this original impetus has the staying power to keep it standing indefinitely.

Put simply, the culture of the West is old. Its primary purpose has been accomplished and over the course of centuries it has assimilated so many contradictory currents that it is sclerotic with the compromises needed to accommodate them all–political compromises, social compromises, economic compromises–accommodations wholly resistant to innovation except in physical technology, however dehumanizing that may become. These compromises might seem essential to quiet the contradictions now that the quest has been accomplished, but they are bringing with them a doom of their own. They have all been worked out in exquisite detail–in custom, in protocol, in law–creating a thicket of intellect through which no vision of the new situation, no decisive action against the unforeseen conundrums that now beset us, is possible. No reform can be made since any reform will put some constituency at a disadvantage. No concern for basic human values is possible because basic human values transcend constituency–being common to us all–and so have no voice in the political struggle. Self-interest demands that each individual attach his or her self to some party or interest group, and fight for its narrow advantage to the exclusion all others. And so does each ensure that all spiral a bit more quickly around the drain of cultural entropy. Of course those who recognize entropy when they see it will realize they must get out of the whirlpool in whatever way possible, even if it requires abandoning the advantages of identifying with any specific faction, and even with the culture itself. By such an escape they lose their leverage in the modern economic machine, and so require some replacement for it. And so I promote the perfection of the art of magick–psychic technology–as a way to gain power that transcends faction, obtain autonomy in any social circumstances, and win a place outside even the most rigid cultural ossification, or most chaotic social disintegration, that history might be able to throw our way.

And perhaps expand such a place until it is a unique space never before recognized on the face of the earth, even though we have been living in it all along.

But then I get ahead of myself here, for I have not explained the logic behind my assertion of cultural decrepitude and, one presumes, rebirth. For this we need a model, a notion of the dynamics of the whole thing, and the one I offer is the cultural morphology of the German historical philosopher Oswald Spengler.

Oswald Spengler (1880-1936) saw cultures as the fundamental historical unit. They are multinational social organisms with life spans of about a thousand years, entities that go through phases of youth, young adulthood, maturity and old age. Upon entering this old age their original purposes will have been largely accomplished, and they begin an indefinite period of senescence that Spengler called "civilization." This marks the end of creative development in the culture and only a slow decline, characterized by pernicious social ossification, can follow. When the civilization becomes brittle enough it cracks and is shattered, and the fragments remain as a raw material for possible incorporation into subsequent cultures.

When the first volume of his *Decline of the West* was published in 1918, Spengler saw the West as well past its maturity, and he believed the only way Germany could flourish was to embrace the reality of the decline and act accordingly. Since a characteristic feature of cultural declines is that one nation in the culture wins the rule over all the others, this caused him to espouse a frankly belligerent German conservativism. Spengler failed in his political efforts, the imperial prize going instead to the United States. But Germany's defeat says nothing about Spengler's model, which held true throughout that contest and during the six decades since as well. Nor was Spengler any sort of Nazi, for he despised their racial theories, their casual brutality, and their political ritual. If he could have had his way, I suspect he would have brought back the Hohenzollerns.

In any case, I find it most convenient to consider him an enlightened reactionary, and treat his historical dynamic as something entirely separate from his politics as a citizen of the Reich. Politics change with each generation, but Spengler's dynamic can be applied to history since the days of the pharaohs. And so I apply it to our current system–the globalized corporate hegemony–to try to explain what ails it.

For Spengler, what causes a culture to age is the gradual ensnarement of Blood by Intellect.

Now Blood for Spengler had no implication of racial purity or any of that claptrap, but was simply life-force, spawning the vision to recognize one's will and the courage to do it regardless of the qualms of those deficient in life-force, who let fear of what might occur inhibit their awareness of what must become. When a culture first comes to birth, there is a surfeit of this imperative force, the impetus that can see an open future and pursues it for the benefit of itself and its line.

Intellect, on the other hand, is the tendency to organize Blood, to restrain it and make it rational, practical, safely in check. Of course even in the culture's freshest youth Intellect is necessary, for Blood must be harnessed if the forms of high culture are to be realized–if a society is to be anything but anarchy. At first this harnessing will be one of custom, of common law more than statutory, but as each accretion builds on the one before, the flow of Blood becomes ever more intellectualized and ultimately attenuated. Now we have a surfeit of lawyers, Blood is only legal in the form of money, and you get the best justice money can buy. In this labyrinth of rationality, there is no room for the expression of power in the sense of *droit*. That can only happen in a culture's youth, when its space is open and the web of rationality not yet strung.

Of course each elaboration of Intellect will be justified as it happens, presented as necessary to the functioning of the system. And so it will be. Each emergency brings a social innovation that ultimately ends up transforming the system as a whole, and invariably it will be an elaboration of Intellect. There were no corporations to speak of, for instance, until railroads were perfected, since their establishment simply required too much capital for one rich man, or a rich family, to pay for the whole thing, and they were too risky to undertake without the protection of limited liability. Once it seemed clear that incorporation worked well for them, every other enterprise wanted the same advantages. And so the vision of the sole proprietor was replaced by the protocols of the commercial institution.

As the culture grows in size and strength, it becomes big and strong enough to bring about catastrophe if the powers encompassed by it are not regulated. To give a late example, the environmental movement is a case in point. In the early years of fervent industrialization—the development which would enable the West to conquer the world–the situation was open enough that environmental considerations could be disregarded without doing irreparable harm. For instance, I have in my possession a chemistry/chemical engineering book printed in 1870. It includes the design of a lead smelter, one which requires that one periodically scrape out the lead accumulating in the stack, for this is where most of it will be recovered, but it entirely disregards all the lead which escapes out the stack to poison the surrounding landscape. In 1870 this was of little consequence in America, the surrounding landscape being largely empty. But the very success of industrialization has filled that landscape with people, and made the value of unpoisoned land too great to jeopardize, and so we have the welter of environmental restrictions that now restrict growth. There is simply not enough space to grow into, neither physical space nor economic nor intellectual. When a culture has reached a certain age, there is no more helping it. The West has reached that point, and it is time to search out something new.

This constriction of the flow of Blood by Intellect applies to organization as well as action. Where once a Carnegie or Vanderbilt could run his company as his personal fief, disregarding all precedent if some opportunity or innovation beckoned, now the commercial world is all bound up in procedure and protocol, with even small, independent businesses tied into it by knots of franchise and contract, all so everyone may take part in the advantages of scale, a scale that now reaches across continents and oceans to embrace the whole globe. Of course the main advantage of scale is simple survival, for without it one will be priced out of the market, unless one can offer something truly new. And within the context of the West, there is nothing new. So what to do when what you came to do has all been done? Make money, of course! Civilizations are complex, finely tuned contrivances for making money, but ultimately unsustainable *because they have no Blood!*

So what happens next? Either a long slide into chaos or the emergence of a new culture.

For Spengler, a high culture is born when an elite subset of the populace recognizes and begins to address a wholly new *type* of **space**. This sort of space will have been hitherto ignored, even though people had been living in it–or perhaps "adjacent to it"–all along. It will offer a particular way of organizing perception, and when the culture is new, its exploration will reveal an undiscovered country to be exploited and dominated. It is the work of accomplishing this conquest that will produce the material, aesthetic, political and social forms that we recognize as the products of high culture.

As each space is unique, so is each culture. A culture may assimilate fragments of past cultures, but only to the extent that these help it actualize its unique realm. A culture's space is a prime symbol. It isn't explicit, no more than water is to a fish, but the culture's whole approach to its circumstances will be based on the unstated assumption that this space is where one finds True Reality. The culture's destiny is thus wrapped up in its conquest of the space. The pursuit of this destiny lends the culture coherence and form until–after about a thousand years–the conquest is complete and satiety replaces all aspiration. A realm of vast potential is replaced by a well-mapped country divided among contending factions that vie for the profits it produces. Then the only motive aside from this pursuit of self-interest is to hold together the disintegrating coherence, even as reality moves into other realms and it becomes obvious that things aren't contained in *just that space* at all.

Obviously all this would be more clear if I gave some examples of these so-called spaces. Though Spengler asserted that there have been eight high cultures so far, he was principally concerned with three–the Classical, the Magian (Byzantine,

Jewish, Persian, Arab, Ottoman), and the Western, which he named the "Faustian." I'll just add his take on the ancient Egyptian for good measure, and that should provide an idea of what he had in mind.

For the Egyptians, life was lived on a linear path from birth to death to rebirth in the afterlife. The model for this space was the linearity of the Nile Valley; Pharaoh was the ruler of upper and lower Egypt, and it was the union of these two segments of the line that inaugurated Egyptian culture. The people received a magickal orientation in this space through the cult of the dead. And the space was given architectural expression through linear temples and tombs, where all was organized around the processional way, the straight line from the entrance to the mummy or god.

Members of the Classical culture organized space with a focus on the immediately present. The political unit was the polis. The aesthetic standard concerned itself with the perfection of the human body, the temple standing on a hill, the euphony of the tuned string. Classical religion was focused around the local cult, with each polis having a patron deity. Greek mathematics was concerned with organizing what could be immediately perceived, whether the relationship of lines drawn in the sand or the motions of the planets. Unseen abstractions, even as basic as the number zero, were not welcome.

For the Magians, destiny was found in a realm wholly abstract: the dogma space delineated by the sacred texts of True Religion, within the span of time between Creation and Apocalypse. The political unit was the Community of Belief, a state which would prosper through the orthodox devotion of its members, and be shattered by heresy and schism.

According to Spengler's reckoning, Faustian culture began around the year 1050, and for it the space to be dominated has been the three dimensions of physical space. The tool that attained this dominion has been physical technology. From musketry to nuclear missiles, from the full-rigged ship to the space shuttle, from the printing press to the Internet, Faustian technics ensures that there can be no place anyplace able to resist its influence. It's architectural imperative emphasizes height–from the gothic cathedral to the skyscraper. The world-wide competition to build ever higher skyscrapers in the most non-Western centers of wealth (e.g., Shanghai, Dubai) is a clear indication that Faustian values have infected the whole world. So its dominion now, for all practical purposes, is an accomplished fact. There is more to be done within this space, of course–nanotechnology, genetic engineering, stem cells–but all will be carried out by institutions operating routinely for the benefit of the institution, according to its mission. For the individual there is no more *quest*, but only a job. The attitude is secure; the subjective "science" space has been dominated. The destiny has been completed, and so a certain ennui has set in.

Events over the last century have only confirmed Spengler's vision. In his scheme, the last centuries of a culture's millennial life-span will be devoted to wars that determine which nation within the culture will claim imperial rule over all the others. For the Classical culture, this was Rome; for the Magians, it was the Ottoman Turks. The 20th century has confirmed this process for the Faustians, with the United States winning this role in spite of the deepest aversion of its populace. And with the establishment of *Pax*

Americana, destiny has been accomplished and there is no further impulse towards it. Desire has become satiety, the psychodynamic equivalent of entropy. But having reached this end-point, there is no further reason to strive for it, and so the coherence that the effort called forth has been lost. And all the cultural artifacts spawned by that effort–everything from its economics to war, the arts and law–lose coherence as well. The culture no longer defends us from the chaos beyond it. It calls chaos up from within itself, and its most picayune internal contradictions can effectively cripple it.

There is no way out of this energetic hole; both the impetus of security and the impetus of profit push us deeper into it.

The Faustian enterprise has reached a conclusion. Without the drive toward destiny that focuses its vigor, its collective current of psychic energy has split itself into millions of separate, disparate and even mutually exclusive personal and corporate interests. With this dissolution of organic unity, only the hard hand of the State remains to ensure political order. Thus do we have the tendency toward "Caesarism," the authoritarian rule that Spengler predicts for the end-stage of "civilization." With the dissolution of cultural coherence, the original, organic political forms of the culture become ever more corrupt and hardened into faction, less able to provide the political coherence needed to accomplish anything. So sooner or later circumstances call up and install a strongman and give him a mandate to sweep aside the partisanship and replace the old forms with his personal vision of good governance. This can work well enough for as long as worthy Caesars succeed one another, but when the chain breaks, it will be reforged in the heat of civil war. Then all is more brittle than before, and more breaks follow, until the whole civilization lies shattered, never to be pieced together again.

But this *could* take centuries. There is still the inertia of the civilization tending to keep things as they were, the momentum of the five billion people who would be dead without it striving to hold its contradictions apart, at least within their minds. But the energy put into their holding apart itself makes the contradictions grow more extreme, until they become inescapable. The system cracks, and in one way or another the chaos beneath it is revealed.

The United States won the great wars of the 20th century, but there is no peace, and no prospect for it anytime soon. War brings no victory, only the illusion of control. Peace means only a further regimentation of the human spirit with hyper-technology and corporate hegemony. It seems the future is incapable of improvement, offering only more crowding and regimentation and more substitution of automation for every kind of honest labor. There will be no further quest to discover Faustian space, only to endure it. When it finally becomes unlivable, the spaces around it–whether empty and open or seething with the resentments of a thousand years–will be so obvious that some may wonder how we could have ignored them for so long. Our vehicle into the future has run out of gas, and we are not alone on the road.

For the present, we are confronted with a question of timing: how long will the Faustian hold together until it becomes unlivable? While in Spengler's view, cultures fulfill their destinies in about a thousand years, civilizations vary in their abilities to endure. The Roman Empire only lasted 400 years. On the other hand, if a civilization is blessed with physical isolation, like ancient Egypt, or if it's big enough and wealthy enough to assimilate its barbarian invaders, like ancient China, it can keep going for millennia.

The Faustian doesn't seem to have such strong legs. Its destiny having been to use physical technics to force the whole world to submit to it, it has no isolation at all, and since any people with money can adopt its technology as well as it can, it has no special advantage there either. All it has is an attitude, and that has gone stagnant. On the other hand, having imposed its gloss on the whole world, the whole world has been contaminated by it, and in one way or another must participate in its fall. Through embracing it as reality, the developing world has tainted its fresh energy with decrepitude. Much is made of the resurgent China, but the natural resources needed for a Faustian rise to greatness are just as depleted for them as they are for us, and our financial systems are intimately linked, they having assimilated the Faustian system with alacrity. They have no new vision to offer, only a billion people who would like to participate in the benefits of material greatness. And so, in essence, they are just as close to the entropic pit as we are.[12] Of course it may take a few hundred years for us all to fall into it–the Faustian is just now entering its time of empire and Caesarism–but then what happens?

One thing that is certain is that without some sort of intervention, the whole Faustian infrastructure will be either wrecked or made irrelevant, vast structures looted or allowed to decay because the power and water needed to make use of them will not be available. And vast amounts of technical knowledge will be lost for much the same reason. And then after some centuries of barbarism a new culture may rise up out of the wilderness and rubble to quest after its own unique destiny. But the easily available resources will all have been used up, so the physical magnificence of the Faustian will be lost to us.

[12] When there is a quest–whether for the conquest of Cultural Space or for something smaller–shortcuts are permitted; *damn the fatalities, full speed ahead!* This was certainly the case in the Faustian sphere up to the mid 20th century, and in a way it's the case in China today, what with their coal mine fatalities, shoddy construction, lead and cadmium in children's toys, melamine in milk and pet food, horrific air pollution, and so on. But their quest is smaller than the original Faustian quest; they simply want to catch up and take their rightful place in the modern, i.e., Faustian world. Thus their efforts offer nothing new, but only another impetus pushing us all closer to the drain.

Unless we begin to spawn the new culture now, within the beginnings of the Faustian decay, the zenith of the human species will have passed. If, however, we can bring a fresh culture to birth within the body of the old, we may use the old infrastructure as a tool to nurture the new while it is still sufficiently intact to be helpful. And there is historical precedent for this process. According to Spengler's reckoning, the Magian culture first came to birth around the year One within the midst of Classical (i.e., Roman) civilization. Though it was distorted at first by the oppressiveness of the Classical forms, it also benefited by being able to continue physically where the Classical left off. Because of this the Eastern Empire never had to suffer from the Dark Ages that the West had to endure, maintaining its prosperity and social vigor until the Magian began to suffer its own decline after the year 1000.

Spengler believed that each culture was unique, standing up on its own and then falling into oblivion without affecting or effecting the cultures that came after. I differ with this formulation, seeing each culture as a stone to step upon as humanity makes its way toward whatever ultimate destiny it may attain, each new culture striving for what is attainable next, given the progress granted by those that came before. And now that the three dimensions of physical space are under our control, we must begin to control ourselves, lest in our passion and despair we use our mastery of matter to destroy ourselves.

Of course in Spengler's scheme, the fundamental work of each culture is to address and conquer a unique sort of space. For Spengler this space is never explicitly acknowledged by those who actually attain the destiny. It remains subliminal, but it is the context for the culture's every achievement. Now that Spengler has revealed all, however, we can no longer remain oblivious to this necessary context. We must address it directly so we might master it while there is still time.

It is in this spirit that I offer *psychic* space as the context for the next culture, wherein we may learn to control the psychic energy and structures of belief that spawn event both within our psyches and beyond them.

3. Cultural Collapse in Terms of Psychic Space

Addressing reality from a standpoint in psychic space requires that we regard the contents of consciousness willfully, using a cold-hearted knowledge of their behavior to manipulate them for the benefit of our purposes, devoid of any passion beyond the aspiration to do our wills. Consciousness cannot be regarded as a window on reality, but must be seen as our tool for managing psychic dynamics so reality manifests in conformity with will.

To deal with psychic space, we must manipulate belief and psychic energy, the matter and motion of the psychic realm. The ideal here is to regard psychic energy not as *what it is*, or how its *genuine aspects* relate to one another, but *how it works*, meaning how *we* can work *it*. Thus may we begin to use it, even to use it reflexively, and a visceral awareness of *what it is* will become innate.

In psychic space, the object of belief takes the place of the physical object. One may protest that objects in matter must conform to physical necessity in order to exist, while we can spawn beliefs willy-nilly, but objects of belief will not persist unless supported by a current of psychic necessity, which at any given moment consists of a flow of desire toward satiety. The object of belief persists only as long as there is a source of psychic energy to animate it; so long as there is, it will be as certain as a rock.

The energetic quality of the present economic situation demonstrates how deenergized belief is inconsistent with duration in psychic or any other sort of space.

In order to animate our ailing economy, sickened by the bursting of the housing bubble, the Doctors of Finance have resorted to the amphetamine of debt, debt more overwhelming than any previously issued except during the crisis of World War Two. And while there was patriotic fervor then–and after that victory, a wealth of productive capacity, and room to grow well out of the debt–now there is only a gray future brightened with a few glimmers of technological breakthrough, but black with scarcity, an aging population, and two billion well-educated developing-worlders who want to be as rich as us.

Debt is intimately tied up with belief–the belief that the borrower is ultimately good for the money–which may be generalized as belief in the promise the future holds. And when it becomes obvious that it doesn't hold much, the belief that "money will come" will be too absurd to justify the expediture of psychic energy needed to sustain it, and the debt will seem like a bad joke. And then all the energy that up until then went into investing the debt with confidence will show itself as a bad job, one's money will vanish, one will be depressed, and so will the economy.

And then the uppers just won't work anymore.

The psychic energy animating any belief is real in and of itself, the motivation of a living metabolism to do its will. But when motivation finds it's been lured by a false promise, it falls into the slough of despond, and chaos laps at the edges. On the other hand, when the motivation is coherent and compelling, it builds order, reality and the future.

Coherence comes from a unity of direction shared by an individual's separate currents of psychic energy, or by its collective flow from a population of individuals. Chaos is a war of all against all. Coherence is found in individual life and small communities and nations as well as in the culture as a whole, and the coherence must be similar on all levels for the whole thing to function smoothly. *The union of the Macrocosm and the Microcosm.*

Coherence is the product of desire focused toward a specific goal. The crux of a high culture is the unity of its expectation. Deep down, the conquest of the space is the shared hope of all. The crux of a stagnating civilization is self-interest. The destined space has been subdued, and all that's left to do is to look out for Number One. Self-interest being the way each individual regards his or her unique self, it's a belief that cannot be held in common at all. The essence might be the same for each believer, but the flow of power in every case is centered inward, so the individual vectors can never merge.

Beliefs can be erected in psychic space in different ways: consciously, subliminally, subliminally willfully contrived (magick), subliminally collectively contrived (religion, politics), and subliminally commercially contrived (advertising, "entertainment"). Subliminal beliefs are invariably more powerful than conscious ones, since we act on them out of habit rather than any sort of decision. Also, energy kept from consciousness acts out on its own in defiance of conscious inhibition. "Conscious desire is non-attractive," as Spare put it. Of course repression of things one would rather not acknowledge gathers power to spawn omens about them, and a deliberate repression of what one wants is the best way to conjure. Thus we have the dynamic behind magickal phenomena. But natural subliminality is as powerful as occult, and as widespread expectation it focuses the mass of psychic energy to create high culture. When the expectations lose their coherence, however, the flow of energy grows diffuse, and even the most venerable forms begin to decay. Exposed as only so many fictions, they are no longer effective at directing psychic energy, and society's long-standing presumption that they were somehow "truth" will have set the stage for anarchy.

There can be no technical fix to any of this, and in fact the advance of technology only hastens the disorder. This of course is entirely at variance with the system's official belief system. Technology is seen by the Powers That Be as the once and future savior of Western culture; all the problems that now confront us, whether of scarcity, inefficiency or education, are seen to be tractable if only the technological fix can be found. But the invariable by-product of more technology is more efficiency. And the more efficiency, the less *necessary* will more humans become, and the more training, conformity and submission will be required for a person to become *necessary*. Also, the more technology, the more specialized will be each technician's task, and the more complete will be its divorce from anything related to the world as a whole. So there will be a technological elite with the ability and pliability to conform to the standards of the corporate mission; the professionals who serve their higher needs (doctors, lawyers, accountants and such); and everyone else. Honest labor in the sense of skilled fabricators will not be required, since all such work will be either automated or else done in the developing world. All the vast majority will have are McJobs, if even them. Nor will individual members of the elite have any certainty or assurance that all their training will have enduring value, so unstable will both the technological landscape and the financial landscape become. You could invest your whole life in acquiring exquisite skill in one tiny technical specialty (skill which has to be exquisite for the technology to work at all), and then the business climate could change, throwing you out of your position. And by the time it changed back, you would be beaten to the new positions by younger, cheaper candidates. For instance, the day before I first wrote this (3 February 2010), Pfizer

Pharmaceuticals announced that it would cut three billion dollars from its research budgets, which translates to at least a billion dollars in salaries–over 10,000 more or less highly skilled people cast into the outer darkness, there to discover what all those years of training were really worth.

One cannot expect such redundant employees to repeatedly reinvest their psychic energy into submission to any social contract. In time such conformity will be replaced by despair, resigned nihilism, crime, cynical bombs of ironic ontology, substance abuse–all conducive to chaos rather than coherence.

By stripping people of any productive autonomy or control, then making them redundant, the system precludes its subjects from participating in a flow of power. Magick offers a way around this prohibition. And it employs a sort of power the system cannot even recognize, and so is the system defenseless against it.

And so magick has a fertile field in which to pull its plow.

This is similar to the dynamic that made the Roman Empire ripe to be subverted by Christianity. The establishment treated the masses like dirt, but the Christians saw the Church–the collective believers–as the body of Christ, each individual to be respected and even nurtured as such. And so it became very attractive as an alternative society, ultimately taking over the State and helping to define two separate high cultures.

In these days when the system requires that we restore it by giving over more and more of our souls, the infinite vistas of psychic space, surging with spirit, look like a refuge indeed. All that is needed is the skill to manage its terrain, and that is just what the art of magick would teach.

4. The Desultory Evolutions of Real Reality

Regrettably, the breakdown of the Faustian arrangement could drag out for centuries, and so we must wonder if there will be anything left of the human spirit once it finally falls in on itself. But it will not be an evenly-distributed breakdown. While the system may abandon some regions of its hegemony in coming decades, others will hold to its order to the last, their populations freezing their souls with the conformity necessary to preserve it, and thinking they are better off for the shedding of the wayward provinces. But they will be possessed by an ever smaller coherence, like a piece of ice in boiling water that is hard enough in its center, but doomed to imminent dissolution.

Of course some people who oppose the corporate hegemony propose that this period of transition be shortened by violent means. They would justify them by citing the pressure on the natural environment and also the sort of creeping emasculation of humanity that the corporate subservience to technology and protocol makes inevitable. One of the more notorious of these violent anarchs is Theodore Kaczynski, author of *Industrial Society and Its Future*. Better known as "The Unabomber Manifesto," this is a close examination of how technology must be unsustainable without a malignant alteration of human nature to accommodate it. Kaczynski felt the situation to be so dire that he blew up technophiles with bombs sent through the mail until the Washington *Post* published his essay, thus gaining it a much larger audience than would otherwise have been possible. And of course it is now freely available on the Internet. So its influence must be far wider than if he hadn't killed people, say if he had instead submitted it to some small anarchist press. Surely I would never have read it, and the fact that I have has caused his thinking to have influenced this essay you are reading here. Of course he paid a price. He now lives in a small cell in the Supermaximum Federal Penitentiary in Florence, Colorado, and the only way he can expect to improve his accommodations is through catastrophic revolution. And he won't get any help on that score from me.

Simply put, I reject Mr. Kaczynski's strategy for action. Violence not only makes you into a target for the annihilating beam of Imperial Power, but it gives the State a certain vigor. Nietzsche's "That which does not kill me makes me grow stronger" applies to the system as a whole as well as to individuals, and such symbolic blows give it the justification and purpose it needs to make its repression ubiquitous. We should recall that the four powers of the Sphinx are to Know, to Dare, to Will and to keep Silence, and bombs sent through the mail are among the loudest sorts of action one can take. If we choose magick as a way to counter our species creeping emasculation, violence must be left out of our arsenal, at least until the crisis point arrives. And I sincerely doubt that point will be reached anytime soon.

What is more important is that we develop our psychic technologies to be able to counter the impetus of the system toward the creation of machine men with an impetus of our own toward the realization of individual divinity. The way to perfect this is to gain the ability to be "occult," or *hidden*, to keep Silence as one goes about the business of attaining one's *own* destiny, rather than conforming to either the acceptable destinies that the system lays out for us or to the ideological imperatives of any fellow-travelers we fall in with as we oppose it. As the system finds itself ever more fractured, it will become ever more vulnerable to infiltration, if only that be uncontaminated with traces of explosives residue and avoids mention on terrorist watch lists. We should keep in mind that for the most part, the intellectuals who serve the system do not acknowledge even the *existence* of psychic energy as an independent stuff,[13] and

[13] Of course neither do many of the aforementioned fellow-travelers, Marxists being atheistic and the political anarchists utterly disdanful of the ontological anarchists, who tend to be sympathetic to the sorcerous attitude.

so is it blind to any sort of psychic action against it. The psychic is a flank to which the minions of the system are wholly oblivious, even as it offers access to the deepest recesses of their lives.

Any sort of system-shattering violence is also unacceptable because so many people would be dead without the system, and those who would break it would bear the guilt of it. Better to have the people who currently run things steer their grand contraption into the ditch, and have the fault themselves.

But there is no reason why we have to stay on board as it hurtles toward chaos.

As I mentioned earlier, Spengler himself offered the possibility that a new culture could grow up in the midst of an aging civilization, recognizing this when the Magian culture emerged in the eastern end of the Roman Empire, thus preserving high culture there until it began itself to fade around 1000. Though the initial forms of the new culture are thus distorted by the old, it has the advantage of being able to appropriate the infrastructure of the aging civilization, gradually replacing it rather than being obliged to start from scratch amidst a field of ruins.

One thing working to advance the possibility of such an immediate substitution now is the fluidity of wealth in Faustian space. Faustian destiny has always focused on leaving the homeland to infest the whole earth with its rapaciousness. But the result here is that loyalty to the homeland is lost. The commerce of the whole world has adopted Faustian finance, and so it has lost all local characteristics. Capital is now multinational and so its interests are, too. And when the economic interests of "everybody" are paramount, this is simply to say that no one's are. "The greater good" is conflated with corporate interest, all loyalty to locality is effaced, connection to soil (and hence Blood) vanishes, and capital becomes wholly intellect, fit to exist solely as zeros and ones in a computer memory.

Capital has loyalty to nation no longer, nor need it have loyalty to culture, either. When it brings itself to move, the transition is instantaneous.

But how can capital move from matter to psyche? Well, how did wealth switch from paganism to Christianity? Basically, it's an exposure of rich people to a rapport with a different way of thinking. In our case it involves making it clear that there is advantage in believing in accordance with will, rather than the other way around. Of course the Faustian order asserts that our notions of belief and psychic energy are hotch-pot and confusion–the end of order–and so it works to suppress them, as much because it fears their ontological implications as any sort of malice or honest incomprehension. In any case, the established system must push the cultural usurper away from the center, into the realm where reside all the other aspects of the old culture that it no longer has power to maintain, regions once Faustian but now something else, arenas of fermentation, chaos and creation quite capable of spawning fresh notions of cultural space.

As the system loses certitude and shrinks in upon itself seeking reassurance, it abandons those realms of social interaction that it can no longer comprehend, yet hasn't the resources to reintegrate. Some of these realms will be physical–think Detroit[14]–but others will be more metaphorical or social. As the decay progresses, the physical regions expand as the establishment turns inward, the metaphorical regions join them, and the process gains momentum. Effective sovereignty over these realms withers away, though should they assert formal independence they will be crushed, since the State retains, in its weakness, the power to annihilate. But the State's loss of rapport with the situation means its day-to-day leverage over life in such realms, though inconvenient and unpleasant for their residents, must ultimately become ineffective. Then the question is, what replaces it?

The ontological anarchist Hakim Bey, in his essay "NoGoZone," gives this question a thorough

[14] Due to the decline of the American auto industry, Detroit has lost half its population since 1960, has a 29% rate of unemployment, and vast stretches of its once-vibrant urban landscape have been abandoned. The current plan is to collect the scattered remnants of the population into more compact neighborhoods and to demolish the remainder for use as greenbelts and farmland, but the city government is close to bankruptcy and so funds from the Federal government will be required to do anything. In decades to come, as more cities follow and the Federal government becomes as impecunious as the local authorities, one might expect abandoned neighborhoods to be allowed to decay at their own pace—a promiscuous creation of NoGoZones, responsibility for the future of which will lie solely with those courageous enough to live in them.

analysis. The obvious answer to our question becomes, "Something must." What it happens to be depends on the skill of those involved, or lack thereof. At the most negative extreme it could be the fascism of drug gangs or the pure thuggery of protection rackets. On the other hand, it could be the enlightened guidance of philosopher kings. But some form of social organization will take over, once the State retreats. Bey points out that historically, the most enduring bonds have been spiritual–religious communities last longer than those inspired by any particular social theory. But to preclude theocracy and the autocracy that always follows, a special sort of religion is required. As Bey puts it:

> I hypothesize the possibility and reality of non-authoritarian, autonomous, self-organized, non-hierarchic aspects of the huge complex subsumed in the word "religion"–shamanism, for example, or the multivalent and infinitely expandable pattern of "paganism," in which no culture can gain a monopoly of interpretation, or even a hegemony. I'm not saying the NGZ should be "religious," I'm saying it will be "religious," and

> is "religious"–and that if we believe in the desire for some liberatory potential in the NGZ, we should begin now to find a "religious" language that will reflect and help to shape and realize that potential–or else we will face a "religion of fascism" (xtian right-wingers attempting to dominate the NGZs) or a spirituality of entropy.

Bey remarks that such a religious practice should see spiritual power as immanent rather than transcendent, be mystical without asceticism, should stress ethics rather than morals, and be radically tolerant on the pagan model. This notion of religion is perfectly suited to the psychic technology called magick, and a very efficient way of introducing refugees from the Faustian to psychic space. Psychic space becomes something to recognize, experience and exploit instead of something to be *granted* a revelation of–since energy pervades psychic space according to its own dynamics, not any human state of grace. Dogma being death to the ability to exploit psychic space, exclusive theism is always inappropriate.

Modern magick–experimental religion at its most audacious–eschews dogma, and in fact calls into question the nature of spiritual belief itself, leaving psychic space wide open. A fundamental theme of modern magick concerns the question of whether there is any such thing as "occult truth" at all. Beyond such facts as the existence of psychic energy, some general tendencies of its behavior, and the more obvious features of the subtle body (e.g. the Kundalini), most modern occultists admit there simply isn't much occult truth out there. But there are a plethora of beliefs and techniques that enable us to organize psychic energy, more or less effectively, and cause it to behave in ways that promote our wills. Thus magicians are as likely to address a belief according to its energy dynamics as they are according to whether they think it "true" or "false." Truth and falsehood are matters of perspective, timing and attitude–easy variables to shift around as needed. But conservation of energy is forever, whether that energy be physical or psychic. Some things are just deeper than belief.

Let me offer a test of whether psychic space can frame the next culture or not: will spiritual organizations in these abandoned realms do best when they manage spirit objectively, or with "true belief?" If the true believers can still succeed in imposing conformity within these regions made "newly free," then maybe humanity is not yet fit to dominate psychic space, unless we need to be purified first with a few centuries' barbarism before people realize that psychic space must be dispassionately addressed.

5. Magick, Religion, Belief, Chaos, Will

In order to operate in psychic space, you need a psychic technology. The two approaches to manipulating psyche that have any traditional record of effectiveness are magick and religion. Spiritual technology starts as magick with shamanism, gains power as religion through the incorporated force–focused through cult practice, law and dogma–of all its believers, but then this very unanimity freezes effective belief and cripples power. Modern magick, on the other hand, seeks to exploit the mechanisms of belief itself. There is no room for dogma here, only for technique and observations of what happens when you use it.

The crux of magickal epistemology is that there can be no way to be certain of the *truth* of any belief within psyche. All we can know about a belief is whether it is *effective* at focusing our psychic energy to do our wills. Thus the symbolic, eschatological, and ontological premises of a religion or system of magick are entirely unprovable, but one's own personal experience and that of one's fellows will inform one as to whether they are effective at everything from lending coherence to one's life to producing effective conjurations or prayers.

Beliefs are appropriate to the context they were designed to address. They can become awkward and even destructive when applied outside of it, or if the context changes and they do not.

Monotheism, for instance, is very effective when you want to weld together a group that has lost its other cohering influences, or never had any to begin with. Aside from uniting the group with custom, ritual and shared expectations, the assumption of the monotheistic attitude will make conflict with other groups more likely, and this will require a strengthening of group solidarity simply in order to survive. And on the psychic planes, faith in a personal god "who has a plan for you" opens a portal for effective magickal working.[15]

On the other hand, monotheistic beliefs are detrimental if you need to tolerate a lot of diversity within your body politic. And with the recent triumph of transportation and communication technology, we're all one world now, and diversity is the operative condition. Thus the belief that people who do not believe precisely as you do are all going to suffer in hell for eternity is no longer effective. We must deal with believers of all sorts, and so we must address the mechanisms of belief itself. This is not a task a religion is equipped to handle. Though often expert in the manipulation of psychic energy, religious practitioners are generally enamored of the prospect of finding the

[15] In essence, if a person has faith that an all-powerful deity has a plan for him, his own future is no part of his concern. In earthly matters, one does one's best and prays. In spiritual matters, one can only pray. But in both cases, in so praying one in fact focuses psychic energy into the desire to be filled. And then, if one has faith, one puts it in God's hands, which is essentially the same thing as what happens when a magician represses all thought of a sigil. And each time a theist thinks about his lack of the prayed-for need, his psychic energy would surge. But he would still continue to subordinate it to God's Plan, which is effectively to repress it again. Eventually, *something* gives way, and the pray is answered.

True Faith in which to believe, and so have no inclination to turn a cold eye on the nature of belief *as such*. Magicians and sorcerers, on the other hand, being instead enamored of the possession of power, are eminently suited to manipulate belief to create whatever webs of power they may need.

This is the epistemological underpinning of the ontological relativism I propounded in Chapter 15 of this book, and it has a great deal of relevance to Spengler's system. That is, how real are the spaces in whose conquest each culture finds its destiny? I would answer that they aren't real at all; they are merely effective fictions. They are subliminal constructions that focus the psychic energy of those who participate in the culture, and so give their actions a coherence that transcends faction and generates all the forms characteristic of that culture. But what of the Faustian space, the three dimensions full of physical stuff? How can this be considered a mere cultural abstraction, a destiny fulfilled and now obsolete? But the stuff itself lies in a different place than the space we have conceptualized and then mastered as a way to dominate it. What we master is our ability to create an accurate model in our minds, a model from which follows procedures for manipulating the stuff, which lies outside our minds and thus outside both our model and the cultural space. The stuff is real, but the only way we can reach it is through the model. This model having been taken to its limit, the contradictions within it have become conspicuous. The space loses its aura of reality and becomes just another way of looking at the whole thing.

"The whole thing," of course, is in the end just the chaos of the natural world and all the energies that move it–physical, psychic and divine. Without the interface of cultural contrivance it is only capable of supporting a few herds of such large beasts as we humans–wandering bands of hunter-gatherers, eventually evolving into tribes, which begin to have a culture of their own, the space being defined by their interaction with the natural order within their territory. What keeps us billions alive today requires something a bit more elaborate, and a lot more abstract, so when faith in its effectiveness–or, anyway, its *completeness*–fades, we don't have raw nature's riches to fall back on, as would a tribal culture. When people discover that the space is no longer complete, a whole realm of unknowable contingency is admitted into any and all deliberations, including the catastrophic–right now mostly involving environmental or financial collapse. Moving through these new contingencies and the socio-political currents that animate them, our much vaunted understanding of matter seems fit only to keep the engine tuned and the chrome polished as we drive our fine contraption over a cliff. There must be laid out a way to map this unknown realm, and psychic space provides a grid against which our discoveries may be referenced. War, financial panic and environmental disaster are more problems of psyche than matter *as such* anyway, and the best way to get some leverage over them is by addressing the realm through which psyche works to make the world.

But then any culture requires a cohering influence, the motif that draws everyone together into the mutual understanding necessary to accomplish anything. And what could that be for something as rooted in the individual as psychic space? Technology that dominates physical space works for everyone and subduing the stuff within it through the Faustian model was a group effort for those who made that culture, just as the Magians united around their communities of belief. And the Classical had the citizens of each polis, united against the barbarians beyond its borders. So what does psychic space offer that can provide for group involvement, and so keep its quest from becoming mere self-interest and self-absorption? Our approach to it must be through our own psyches, and we will find the phenomena within them wholly subjective. What is there to share here?

But even if a culture is wholly devoted to matter, its members can still only live within their own heads, bound to the subjective, never to escape. The only thing that makes psychic space different in this regard is that it emphasizes this subjective bias, and provides avenues for accommodating it in practice. And what do we find in this subjective realm, what phenomena with which we might weave an overspreading coherence? Our own psychic energy, to be sure, but also the psychic energy that emanates from every other psyche that is aware within our spheres of awareness–human, animal, elemental, or even divine–energy which intrudes into our individual psychic spaces and must be dealt with in one way or another. And mightn't it be possible that these separate energies so ceaselessly mixing could be brought into a harmony, each responding to the feedback of the others, generating a psychic equilibrium that could weave a web of coherence, a fabric of interlocking intent fit to wrap up the most unruly chaos and subdue it to the purpose of high culture?

Only if those with a free will to follow choose to cultivate such a harmony.

This requires a measure of discipline, a mastery of psychic energy, and the insight into self to realize what one must do to be oneself, and then do it in spite of the siren call of one's lower appetites. And the need for such discipline is consistent with Spengler's cultural model. For him cultures begin when an elite within a population recognizes a previously unacknowledged space and endeavors to dominate it. These people form the aristocracy of the culture, and in the past this has always been an aristocracy of arms, its members being those with the physical and mental prowess to dominate their chosen space. Prowess at arms having been made obsolete in our modern age of annihilating tools of war, I propose an aristocracy of spirit, open to any willing to dominate psychic space, beginning with that within their selves, regarding their passions and prejudices as a fuel for will rather than indications of necessity. As for those incapable of such discipline, well, "the slaves shall serve."

That last quotation brings us back to Chapter 17 of this book, as it is from *Liber AL vel Legis*, "The Book of the Law." The implication, of course, is that only those who can master the law can expect to master themselves. The whole of the law is, of course, "Do what thou wilt," so I should distinguish this imperative from the self-interest characteristic of cultural decline that I mentioned back in Section Three. You will recall that I asserted that self-interest is useless as a cohering force in a society because though the essence of it might be the same for each person, the flow of power "is in every case centered inward, so the individual vectors can never merge." But the action consequent to "Do what thou wilt" is the exact opposite of this. The flow of power does not go from the outside into the center, but from the center out into the world–the "little sister" of Nuit, Our Lady of the Stars–searching out the best way to unite with her, and as each individual pushes out, he or she is prodded in return. Again, the model for human interaction here is that of stars in a galaxy–"Every man and every woman is a star"–where the only obligation of each is to respond to the gravity of all the others. To the extent their motions stay true to an orbit around the galactic center of mass, so will they in their collective motion fall without interference. When they stray from these destined courses, however, they must necessarily drag their neighbors out of theirs, and so the perfect spiral becomes a jumble of chaos and collision. Thus Crowley stresses that everyone who finds their will and does it helps everyone else to do the same. The important thing is to begin.

One fine place to start is through the attainment of mental Silence. Except when we need to attend to detailed plans, and mental speech is meant to remind us of the steps necessary to carry them out, generally when we talk to ourselves it is one or another of our particular spirits or demons defining the world for us according to its special agenda. Whether grand or petty, such agendas are always limited, and so have only an ancillary relationship to True Will. But such limited actors may speak only when they have the energy to do so, and so when they are speaking you have energy available to take–whether to store it or use it for something useful–rather than just letting it assert its narrow vision of what's going on. That is, it's easy enough to synthesize spirits capable of transforming the energy that animates them into whatever sort of psychic energy you require. Once this is done, the actor's speech is silenced. If you have the perseverance to silence them all, you will be freed to perceive and respond to the pure impulse of True Will, which acts from behind speech, through Inspiration and Necessity, not through the rationalizations speech is so wont to produce.

Stephen Mace

27 February 2010

About the Author

Stephen Mace is a heretical chaos magician living in Connecticut. He considers himself a chaos magician because he is a committed believer in the Butterfly Effect, and he has a strong affinity for the magick of Austin Osman Spare. He considers himself to be heretical because he holds to the efficacy of the Holy Guardian Angel as a tool a magician may use to manage his or her spiritual swarm. For the past 49 years he has been working at perfecting the technique for managing his own swarm, and also the psychic energy that animates it and everyone else's. He has done his best to explain this technique in seven books, among them *Shaping Formless Fire, Taking Power* and *Seizing Power*, all published by New Falcon Publications.

As one might expect, portions of these cover politics as well—political processes being the prime exemplars of exoteric psychic dynamics, and the arena wherein the esoteric, personal currents of power must play out. Fortunately, beyond them both there is the play of nature and the universe, and the connection to these seems to be intrinsically better for the personal than for the political. Let us work to make it so.